Handel House Museum Companion

Jacqueline Riding

Donald Burrows
Anthony Hicks

Any copy of this book issued by the publisher as a paperback is sold subject to the condition that it shall not by way of trade or otherwise be lent, resold, hired out or otherwise circulated without the publisher's prior consent in any form of binding or cover other than that in which it is published and without a similar condition including these words being imposed on a subsequent purchaser.

First published in the United Kingdom in 2001 by
The Handel House Trust Ltd
25 Brook Street
London W1K 4HB

© 2001 The Handel House Trust Ltd

All Rights Reserved. No part of this publication may be reproduced or transmitted in any form or by any means, electronic or mechanical, including photocopy, recording or any other information storage and retrieval system, without prior permission in writing from the publisher.

British Library Cataloguing-in-Publication Data
A catalogue record for this book is available from the British Library

ISBN: 0-9541670-0-7
D.L.: M-45.437-2001

Edited by Jacqueline Riding
Designed by Isambard Thomas
Produced in Spain by Turner Publicaciones, S.L.

FRONT COVER Detail of the opening of the Hallelujah Chorus from Handel's autograph score. Handel House Collections Trust.

BACK COVER John Buckler, *Handel's House*, watercolour, 1839. Handel House Collections Trust.

TITLE PAGE View of the 'Rehearsal and Performance' room from the staircase, No. 25 Brook Street. Photograph, Matthew Hollow.

P.6 The bedroom, No. 25 Brook Street. Photograph, Matthew Hollow.

P.88 The 'Rehearsal and Performance' room, No. 25 Brook Street. Photograph, Matthew Hollow.

PICTURE CREDITS

Figs. 14, 26, 74 by permission of the British Library, London.

Fig. 28 courtesy of Country Life Magazine.

Fig. 9 © The Dean and Chapter of Westminster Abbey, London.

Fig. 25 © English Heritage Photo Library.

Figs. 18–20, 22 © George Garbutt, Photography

Figs. 3, 8, 11, 49, 50 © Guildhall Library, Corporation of London.

Illustrations for title page, opposite preface, back page, back cover and figs. 2, 4, 7, 10, 13, 30, 31, 33, 39, 40, 43–45, 52–63, 67–72 © The Handel House Trust Ltd.

Fig. 41 by permission of London Borough of Lambeth Archives.

Figs. 15–17 by permission of the London Metropolitan Archive, Corporation of London.

Fig. 66 by kind permission of Lord Malmesbury and the Trustees of the Viscount FitzHarris 1969 Settlement.

Figs. 1, 5, 6, 29, 34–36, 51, 64 by Courtesy of the National Portrait Gallery, London.

Fig. 27 by permission of Norfolk Museums Service (Norwich Castle Museum).

Fig. 42 The Royal Collection © 2001, Her Majesty Queen Elizabeth II.

Fig. 12 by kind permission of the Survey of London.

Figs. 32, 37, 38, 54 © Tate, London 2001.

Fig. 46 © Victoria and Albert Museum Picture Library.

Figs. 47, 48, 65, 73 by permission of the Victoria and Albert Museum.

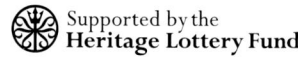
Supported by the Heritage Lottery Fund

Preface STANLEY SADIE	7
Chapter 1: George Frideric Handel DONALD BURROWS	8
Chapter 2: Handel's House JACQUELINE RIDING	20
Chapter 3: Handel's London JACQUELINE RIDING	36
Chapter 4: Handel the Man JACQUELINE RIDING	48
Chapter 5: Rehearsal and Performance JACQUELINE RIDING	62
Chapter 6: Composition ANTHONY HICKS	74
Index	86
Acknowledgments	87

Preface

It was in 1959 – when a party was given in the house by Viyella, who then occupied it, to commemorate the bicentenary of Handel's death – that it first struck me that No. 25 Brook Street ought to honour, in some permanent way, the memory of its first and most notable occupant. But nothing could be done about it for more than thirty years: it was not until the beginning of the 1990s that Julie Anne Sadie and I made the first moves to set up the Handel House Trust and to establish a museum in the house.

Historically, composers seem to have been remarkably mobile people. There are extraordinarily few examples across the history of music of a composer staying in the same premises for more than a quite brief period, and almost none from the eighteenth century, when people in general moved house much more often than they do today. Often their careers demanded mobility. Few of Handel's contemporaries, especially those who dwelt in the world of opera, were of fixed abode for more than a few years at a time. So No. 25 Brook Street is not far from being unique in being a great composer's chosen dwelling for as much as thirty-six years.

It was in 1723 that Handel chose to live there. Until that time, he had chiefly lived – as far as we know – in the houses of friends and patrons. Now he chose to be by himself, with his own establishment and his own servants. It was a key moment in his career. He held an annual pension of £400 in his role as music master to the royal family. He was musical director of the opera company, the Royal Academy of Music (which perhaps seemed more secure a position than it actually turned out to be). He had newly been appointed as Composer to the Chapel Royal. His situation in English society was assured, and it was a situation superior, it seems, to that occupied by even the most senior of native composers. He mixed in higher levels of society than they – as his choice of residence in a new, fashionable, upper-middle class area indicates – and he was usually known as 'G.F. Handel, Esq.' rather than 'Mr G.F. Handel'.

Taking No. 25 Brook Street was, then, a statement about his plans for the future. He rented the house rather than buying – as a foreign national, he could not own property in 1723; he could have done so when four years later he was naturalized, but he still preferred to be a tenant rather than owner. Perhaps he valued the flexibility – and indeed there were once rumours, around 1740, that he was contemplating a return to Germany. But No. 25 Brook Street was where he remained, where he wrote his greatest music, and where in 1759 he died. It is proper that we should value and preserve it, and that his music should echo in his house once again.

STANLEY SADIE

George Frideric Handel

DONALD BURROWS

fig.1 [previous page]
Francis Kyte, *G F Handel*,
oil on canvas, 1742, 194 × 168mm.

National Portrait Gallery, London.

fig.2
Johann Jakob Haid after Johann Salomon Wahl, *Johann Mattheson*, mezzotint engraving, n.d., 317 × 191mm.

Private collection.

WHEN HANDEL FIRST came to London in 1710 the twenty-five year old composer brought with him a wealth of experience, both professional and personal. In Halle, the German city of his birth (23 February 1685) he had received his initial training from the organist, Friedrich Wilhelm Zachow (1663–1712) and his first musical post was as organist at Halle's Calvinist Domkirche (1702). From probably as early as 1701, Handel established regular contact with the composer Georg Philipp Telemann (1681–1767) in Leipzig. In Hamburg (1703–5/6) he had worked at the opera house, initially under Reinhard Keiser (1674–1739), first as an orchestral violinist and then as a harpsichordist. At the Hamburg Opera, Handel also formed a competitive friendship with tenor singer and composer Johann Mattheson (1681–1764) (fig.2), which at one stage resulted in a duel over who should direct the orchestra. In Italy (1705/6–10) his operas had been performed in Florence (*Rodrigo* 1707) and Venice (*Agrippina* 1709–10), he had enjoyed success with Italian cantatas and Latin church music in Rome, and also with his first oratorios, *Il trionfo del Tempo e del Disinganno* (1707) and *La Resurrezione* (1708), the latter written under the patronage of the Marquis Ruspoli (the orchestra was led by the great violin virtuoso Archangelo Corelli). Handel seems to have had some engaging qualities which, aided (as we may suppose) by some diplomatic skills, led him to rapid acceptance at the centres of power: thus he levered himself into directing opera performances at Hamburg (including his first opera, *Almira* in 1704/5), achieved the patronage of the Cardinals Pamphili and Ottoboni soon after his arrival in Rome, was commissioned to write *Aci, Galatea e Polifemo* for the wedding of the Duke of Alvito at Naples in 1708 and, in 1710 when he decided to turn his career northwards again from Italy, the Elector of Hanover (Georg Ludwig) virtually re-created the dormant post of *Kapellmeister* in order to secure his services. His personal charisma seems to have been enhanced by his skills as a keyboard player: the Dowager Electress of Hanover described him as 'quite a handsome man' who 'plays marvellously on the harpsichord'. Within a few months of his arrival in London he had performed before Queen Anne at St James's Palace.

Handel's removal to London had both a professional and a political aspect. He came initially to compose for the fledgling London theatre company that was presenting Italian operas at the recently-completed Queen's (later King's) Theatre in the Haymarket (fig.3): his desire to become more consistently involved with an opera company was matched by the London company's need for a composer. His first London opera, *Rinaldo* (performed 1711) was well received, and the experience no doubt persuaded Handel that he had a promising future in London. Even so, at that stage he probably did not foresee that the city would become his permanent home. He had originally come to London on a year's leave of absence from his post at Hanover, and it was well known that, unless there was significant Jacobite intervention† the Hanoverian family was in line for succession to the British crown upon the death of Queen Anne, the last Stuart monarch. It was probably useful for the Hanover court to have Handel as an advance cultural representative in London (to which he returned in 1712) and the succession of his Hanoverian employer as King George I in 1714 (fig.5) was a key factor in establishing Handel's permanent career.

The story of that career was dominated by the changing fortunes of Handel's theatrical enterprises – in Italian opera up to 1741, and overlapping with English oratorio, which dominated the composer's

fig.3
William Capon, *The Queen's Theatre, later the King's Theatre, Haymarket.* watercolour, c.1783, 182 × 210mm.
Guildhall Library.

† The "Jacobites" were the supporters of the claim to the British throne of the deposed King James II's male line.

fig.4 [opposite]
Title page, *Arie dell' Opera di Rinaldo, &c*, printed score, pub. John Walsh senior and John Hare, 1711, London.

Handel House Collections Trust.

fig.5
Studio of **Sir Godfrey Kneller, Bt**, *King George I,* oil on canvas, 1714, 756 × 635mm.

National Portrait Gallery, London.

later years. There were other important elements, however. During his early years in London, Handel made a big impression with orchestrally-accompanied English church music: the Te Deum and Jubilate for the state celebration of the Peace of Utrecht in July 1713, which took place in St Paul's Cathedral, another of London's interesting new buildings. His ceremonial style came to prominence again in his anthems for the coronation of King George II and Queen Caroline in 1727, which included the celebrated *Zadok the Priest*. Other pieces of English church music on a less grand scale run as an occasional thread through his career: these include pieces as diverse as the anthem *As pants the Hart* and the setting of Charles Wesley's hymn 'Rejoice, the Lord is King'. Many works were the result of his association with the Chapel Royal to which he received a court appointment as Composer in 1723. There was also an important strand in instrumental works. Some of these were 'public' music, such as the Op. 6 concertos and the organ concertos which were performed with his theatre works, or the *Water Music* (1717) and *Music for the Royal Fireworks* (1749), the latter attracting Handel's largest audience ever at its open-air rehearsal in Vauxhall Pleasure Gardens and the performance in Green Park (see fig.40, p.46).

It is much more difficult to place the biographical context for his keyboard music and instrumental sonatas: while Handel's public career in theatre and church is well documented, we know little of his private and recreational activities. We may reasonably guess that he spent a large proportion of his off-duty time with other professional musicians, with musically-interested amateurs and, perhaps on a more formal basis, with influential patrons, but we do not know whether, for example, the keyboard suites reflect private performances or a personal interest that was developed in isolation. While we can document the periods of Handel's composition and performances each year with considerable accuracy – even down to knowing what he did on each day of the week – there are also periods when he vanishes from the documentary record. We know of his occasional visits to continental Europe for various reasons – to put performers under contract for the opera company, to recover his health at Aix-la-Chapelle in 1737, and to make contact with associates or his family – of two visits to Bath and Tunbridge Wells and of one trip each to Scarborough and Salisbury: there may have been other visits to the 'country' in Britain, though from the time that he moved into his Brook Street house in 1723 his only extended period of absence from London was his visit to Dublin between November 1741 and August 1742. In the summer of 1733 he gave a short series of oratorio performances at Oxford, during the University's degree-giving season, though he did not receive a degree himself.

As time went on it would have become increasingly difficult for Handel to re-develop his career in another place on continental Europe, especially after his naturalisation as a British subject in February 1727. Nevertheless, his career in London, which spanned nearly half a century, was neither predictable nor stable. During 1712–15 he composed *Il pastor fido*, *Teseo* and *Amadigi* for the opera house and may have lived for a time at the Piccadilly mansion of Richard Boyle, Earl of Burlington (1694–1753). However, London's first Italian opera company proceeded on a rather hand-to-mouth basis, with no financial security: a political row within the Royal Family in 1717 (a common occurrence for the Hanoverian dynasty) split the patronage base and precipitated the permanent closure of the company, which had become financially unviable by then in any case. For the following few years London had nothing substantial to offer Handel, and, mirroring his earlier patronage in Italy, it is at this time (1717–18) that he worked for James Brydges, Earl of Carnarvon (1674–1744) (subsequently Duke of Chandos), composing *Acis and Galatea* and *Esther* for private performance, and eleven chamber-scale anthems (the Cannons or "Chandos" Anthems) and a Te Deum, which were performed at the Church of St Lawrence adjoining Brydge's estate at Cannons in Edgware. During this time he also seems to have composed or revised the music of his keyboard suites (including the movement that became known as 'The Harmonious Blacksmith'), which were published in 1720. By 1719 plans were afoot to set up a more well-regulated opera company, the Royal Academy of Music, to which Handel was appointed 'Master of the Orchestra', though he seems in practice to have been the leading composer and impresario. The Academy was set up as a joint-stock company with a term of 25 years: in fact the Academy's financial resources only managed to support nine seasons between 1720 and 1728, but even so this represented the most stable long-term institution in London's operatic history. In the early years Handel did not have uninhibited artistic freedom within the company, because he was in a situation of some competition with the company's other composers, in particular Giovanni Bononcini (1670–1747). By 1723–4, however, Handel had emerged as the undoubted artistic leader. It was at this period that he moved into his house in Brook Street, and in which he composed some of his greatest operas, commencing with *Giulio Cesare* and *Tamerlano* (1724). When the Academy found that it could not proceed any further on the original basis in 1728, he took over the

fig.6
Elisha Kirkall after Joseph Goupy, *Senesino (Francesco Bernardi)*, mezzotint engraving, n.d., 262 × 221mm.

National Portrait Gallery, London.

fig.7
Title page, *Julius Caesar: An Opera*, printed score, 1st ed., pub. John Cluer, 1724, London.

The Byrne Collection,
Handel House Collections Trust.

management of the subsequent seasons on his own account, in partnership with the Swiss impresario John James Heidegger (1666–1749), who was then manager of the King's Theatre.

That arrangement survived for about five years and was eventually broken up because of pressure from a new opera company, the Opera of the Nobility, which was formed in opposition to Handel's company by a new generation of opera patrons, encouraged by Handel's early patron Burlington, and Frederick, Prince of Wales (1707–51). Nearly all of Handel's singers, including the castrato Senesino (Francesco Bernardi) (d. by 1759) (fig.6), defected to the other company, and with the arrival of the celebrated castrato Farinelli (Carlo Broschi) (1705–82) to join the new company, the future of Handel's opera career appeared to be on very shaky ground. However, he set up for a period with his own company at the new, rather smaller, Covent Garden Theatre under the management of John Rich (1692–1761) (*Ariodante*, 1734/35 and *Alcina*, 1735 were both first performed there) (fig.8). In 1732, at the end of his period at the King's Theatre, Handel had introduced performances of an English oratorio, *Esther*, on the end of his English opera season, and in the 1730s he developed both operas and oratorios: his oratorio-type works from this period included *Athalia*, *Alexander's Feast*, *Saul* and *Israel in Egypt*. There was no even pattern, however, because Handel's programmes from season to season were defined by his resources, and in particular his solo singers. It was at Covent Garden in 1735 that he first introduced organ concertos into performances of the oratorios, as interval music or overtures. The London theatre-going public was not sufficient to support two opera companies, and by 1737 it was clear that something had to be done. For one season (1737–8) Handel wrote operas (most notably *Serse*) to commissions from the new opera patrons at the King's Theatre but he apparently did not find this to be a happy arrangement, and in 1739–41 he returned to giving seasons on his own account, taking the rather modest theatre at Lincoln's Inn Fields.

fig.8
Unknown engraver (William Hogarth?), *Rich's Glory or his Triumphant Entry into Covent-Garden*, engraving, 1811 (re-issue), 169 × 309mm.

Guildhall Library.

Here, in 1739–40, he gave his first full all-English season which included the first performances of *L'Allegro, il Penseroso ed il Moderato* and the *Song* [*Ode*] *for St Cecilia's Day*, and in 1740–1 his last season of Italian opera in London. The Dublin visit, where *Messiah* was first performed to great acclaim, marked a caesura in Handel's career, and at that stage he probably recognised that he had no future with Italian opera in London.

This did not mean, however, that Handel was confident about the future direction of his London career. In 1743 his first attempt at an English oratorio season after his return from Dublin was encouraging, with considerable success in a run of performances of *Samson* – as Horace Walpole (1717–97) noted: 'Handel has set up oratorio against the opera, and succeeds'. The success of *Samson* perhaps compensated Handel for the surprisingly lukewarm reception that *Messiah* was given in London during the same season. In many ways the next two seasons, one at Covent Garden and one at the King's Theatre, saw him at the height of his powers, with ambitious programmes of oratorio-style works, but they were made difficult by obstruction and resentment from the 'opera party' led by Lord Middlesex (1711–59). We can only guess what the long-term consequences might have been, because London's life was next disrupted by the second Jacobite rebellion of 1745 (led by the flamboyant Stuart, Bonnie Prince Charlie), sending the troubles of public entertainments into the background. To a large extent Handel's recovery of his own situation was attributable to the success in 1747 of *Judas Maccabaeus*, an oratorio with strong patriotic overtones written in honour of William, Duke of Cumberland (1721–65), the victor at the decisive Battle of Culloden (16 April 1746) which effectively destroyed the Jacobite cause.

From 1747 Handel settled into the pattern of regular Lenten oratorio seasons that was to serve for the rest of his career, at the same time abandoning the old opera-derived structure of subscription seasons in favour of individual tickets for each performance. He developed an annual routine, which usually involved the composition of one or two new scores in the period directly after the completion of the oratorio season, though two new influences, one positive and one negative, were to produce further changes within a few years. In 1749 he began his association with the Foundling Hospital, a new charity (founded 1739) dedicated to the care of abandoned children, by giving a concert which attracted considerable social attention, and followed hard on the heels of his popular exposure through the *Fireworks Music*. From 1750 onwards he gave *Messiah* annually in the Hospital's chapel as a series of charity performances: the effect of this was to establish *Messiah* as his most popular oratorio, and incidentally to confirm Handel's position as a London public figure who was well-known outside the world of the theatre. In 1751 the composition of the oratorio *Jephtha* was severely interrupted by problems with Handel's eyesight, and over the next few years this deteriorated into total blindness, putting an end to his composition career, but also affecting the practicalities of his direction of musical performances. His former pupil, the composer John Christopher Smith the younger (1712–95) – son of Handel's principal copyist John Christopher Smith the elder (1683–1763) – was summoned back from a visit to continental Europe in order to deal with the latter aspect.

In his last years Handel seems to have become something of a recluse, apart from his continuing attendance at oratorio seasons, in which he still occasionally played organ solos. Nevertheless, in May 1756 one friend recorded meeting him at the house of Charles Jennens (1700–73) (librettist of *Messiah*) 'quite blind, but pretty cheerful, & after dinner play'd fine on Mr Jennen's piano forte'. The last codicil to his will signed three days before his death on 14 April 1759, included a wish that 'I hope to have the permission of the Dean and Chapter of Westminster to be buried in Westminster Abbey', and indeed this was fulfilled: the career émigré of 1710 had become a respected and celebrated Londoner.

fig.9
Louis François Roubiliac, *Monument to Handel*, marble, c.1759–62.
Westminster Abbey.

Handel's House

Jacqueline Riding

The House in Lower Brook Street (at present, 1839, numbered 57), in which Handel lived and died; as it appeared before the front of the Attic Story was raised.

fig.10 [previous page]
John Buckler, *Handel's House*, watercolour, 1839, 401 × 316mm.

Handel House Collections Trust.

The inscription reads, 'The House in Lower Brook Street (at present, 1839, numbered 57), in which Handel lived and died – as it appeared before the front of the attic story [sic] was raised.'

HANDEL MOVED INTO what is now No. 25 Brook Street during the summer of 1723, encouraged no doubt, by his court appointment as Composer to the Chapel Royal earlier that year. As far as is known, this was the first London house which Handel had occupied in his own right. Perhaps with his career seemingly secure, and at the age of thirty-eight, Handel felt it was time to have his own space. He was the first occupant of the house, which formed part of a four-building residential development by the speculative builder George Barnes (Nos. 23, 25, 27/29 and 31, the last no longer exists). Brook Street, which connects Hanover Square in the east to Grosvenor Square in the west, was planned and built between 1717 and 1726. As a foreign national, Handel could not own property or take a long lease. After his British naturalisation in 1727, Handel's circumstances changed (No. 25 was probably not available for purchase) but he clearly decided to remain at Brook Street, renewing a short-term lease, as did his immediate neighbours. When he moved in, these were a Mrs Catherine Johnson at No. 23 (soon succeeded by Sir John Avery and then Colonel Henry Hunt of the Guards) and John Monckton, Member of Parliament and later first Viscount Galway, at No. 27/29. As the social status of his neighbours reveals, this was a good, upper-middle class area, at a discrete distance from the music and artist communities centred around Soho and Covent Garden but near to St James's Palace, where he performed his official duties, and the King's Theatre in the Haymarket, the focus of his Italian opera career at this time.

The plan of the house was usual for a modest London townhouse of the period. There was a basement containing the kitchens; from ground to second floor level, a front and back room with a small closet block at the rear (fig. 12); and garrets at the top. The passage from the front door led to the "dog-leg" staircase at the back. Prior to his move, Handel would probably have ordered his basic furniture – including a bed – which may have been new or good quality second-hand. If he owned instruments at this point, it can also be assumed that he personally supervised the moving of them as well as the ordering of

fig.11 [opposite]
Detail showing Brook Street (centre left), St. James's Palace (bottom) and the Haymarket (centre right) from George Foster, *New and Exact Plan of the Cities of London and Westminster…*, 1738.

Guildhall Library.

fig.12
John Sambrook, *Plans of Handel's House, No. 25 Brook Street, Mayfair, as built 1721–2*.

Survey of London.

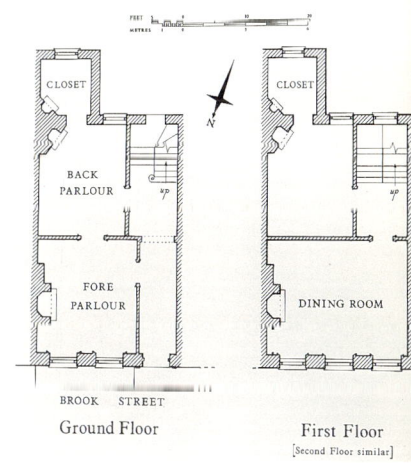

Ground Floor — First Floor [Second Floor similar]

fig.13 [opposite]
Jacobus Houbraken, after an unknown original, *Handel*, surround and scene underneath after Hubert Francois Gravelot, engraving, 1738, 356 × 221mm.

Handel House Collections Trust.

This print was issued to subscribers to the score of *Alexander's Feast* and is the only portrait print known to have been published with Handel's approval.

curtains, window seats and bed hangings of appropriate quality and design. The first floor would have been the main reception/entertaining rooms. The front room, as the largest in the house, probably contained at least one of Handel's larger instruments (a harpsichord and a "little" house organ). It is therefore likely that this is where rehearsals took place (see chapter 5). The adjoining room is believed to have been Handel's main composing room (see chapter 6). The second floor contained the main bedroom at the front with a dressing room at the back, whilst the servants (numbering at least three towards the end of his life) slept in the garrets. Aside from living, sleeping, entertaining, composing and rehearsing, Handel also conducted some business from his Brook Street residence. For the score of *Alexander's Feast* an advertisement dated 15 June 1737 announced that 'Subscriptions are taken in by the Author, in his House in Brook-Street, Hanover Square' and later on 11 March 1738, *The Craftsman* announced that 'MUSICK, this Day is Publish'd, And ready to be deliver'd to the Subscribers, by the Author, at his Brook-Street house, Hanover Square.' Such visitors would probably have been ushered into the ground-floor front parlour by one of Handel's servants.

By the time of his death, all available wall-space on the main floors of Handel's house (possibly even the stairwell) must have been covered with fine art, as is indicated by the sale catalogue of 28 February 1760 (Frick Art Library, New York) which lists over eighty paintings, predominantly oils, plus prints. Some of the prints were probably framed, whilst others were displayed in portfolios. It is likely that the closets contained the smaller "cabinet" pictures such as "A Conversation with Boors" by Teniers and the Watteau conversation piece. In addition to the paintings listed in the catalogue, Handel's will records a number of paintings including two Rembrandts, which were bequeathed to his friend Bernard Granville (1689–1775). A Rembrandt landscape was acquired by Handel in 1749/50 for £39.18s (in 1742 his annual rent for Brook Street was £50). He also owned at least one portrait of himself; the portrait by Philip Mercier (1689–1760) (painted in *c.*1730) was

fig.14
An Inventory of the Household Goods of George Frederick Handel Esqr: Deceased taken at his Late Dwelling House in Great Brook Street St Georges Hanover Square & By Order of the Executor sold to Mr Jno Du Bourk this Twenty Seventh of Augt 1759 …
(last page), manuscript.
British Library (Egerton 3009.E., ff, 1-18).

fig.16 [opposite, above]
First floor front room in 1985.
London Metropolitan Archive.

fig.17 [opposite, below]
Second floor front room
(the bedroom) in 1985.
London Metropolitan Archive.

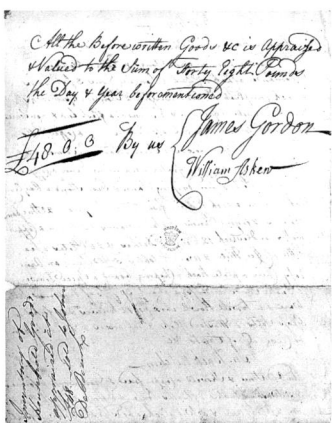

fig.15
Exterior of No. 25 Brook Street in 1944.
London Metropolitan Archive.

in Handel's possession until around 1748, when he gave it to his friend Thomas Harris (1712–85). The portrait remains in the family's collection.

After Handel's death in April 1759, the tenancy passed to his servant John Du Burk, who not only inherited all of Handel's clothes but purchased for the sum of £48 the chattels which remained in the house in the August after the composer's death (fig.14). Du Burk lived in the house until 1772 and may have run it as a boarding house, which explains why he purchased the remaining furniture, including four beds. Around 1790, the closets at the rear were replaced by a bow-window block. It may have been during this re-modelling that some of the panelling was removed. Aside from the raising of the garrets to a full storey during the 1830s, the house remained relatively undisturbed until 1905 when the art dealer C J Charles turned what was still a house into a shop. His "conversion" included the removal of the entire original façade up to second floor level and all existing internal partition walls (fig.15). His justification was that West End property was 'far too valuable to be left to rot because some genius of a past age happened to have lived in a particular spot at one time.' From 1910, the house was occupied by Charles Tozer (an interior decorater) and his successors until 1975 (in 1953–4 the first floor façade was re-instated) and afterwards by antique dealers (figs.16 and 17). Since 1971 the freehold has been owned by the Co–operative Insurance Society.

It was agreed prior to the Handel House Trust leasing the property in 2000 that, where possible and appropriate, the interiors should be returned to the early Georgian period. This decision was based upon the fact that the building's Grade I listing was through its association with Handel. In addition, the refurbishment of the "space" occupied by Handel was deemed appropriate due to the existence of the original staircase, with its exquisite tread ends. To return the floor plans of the front and middle (originally the back) rooms on the first and second floors to their early Georgian sequence, later partition walls were removed and where required, walls were reinstated. To return the fabric of the interiors to as close as possible to their 1720s appearance, the

27

HANDEL'S HOUSE

fig.18 [right]
The staircase at No. 25 Brook Street before restoration.

fig.19 [top]
A tread end.

fig.20 [above]
New panelling for the stairwell being made at Hannaford's workshop.

Trust used the adjoining No. 27/29 Brook Street – part of the original Barnes development and retaining (ironically perhaps) much of its period detail – as the prototype for panelling profiles, cornices, shutters, dados and window seats. Three marble fire surrounds salvaged from the early eighteenth-century Tom's Coffee House in Russell Street, Covent Garden, were installed in the front and middle rooms on the first floor and the bedroom (figs. 21 and 22). The floors were patched in with second-hand boards, which were limed and waxed, and lime plaster ceilings were reinstated.

After extensive analysis, 1720s paint samples were found on the original panelling at the upper floor level and stairwell, and on an original door on the second floor (figs. 23 and 24). The door had an extraordinary twenty-eight layers of paint. In both cases the first layer was "lead" or grey. Analysis in the adjoining No. 23 Brook Street also revealed grey as the first layer. On the original panelling in No. 25, the "lead" colour was covered with a thick layer of grease and dirt, suggesting that there had been no subsequent re decoration for a

fig.21 [above]
One of the Tom's Coffee House fire surrounds in situ at Russell Street, Covent Garden.
Photograph, Dan Cruickshank.

fig.22
The fire surround relocated in the first floor front room of No. 25 Brook Street..

fig.23
Detail of original panelling in No. 25 Brook Street (third floor, originally the garrets).
Photograph, Patrick Baty.

fig.24
Original door on the second floor of No. 25 Brook Street.
Photograph, Patrick Baty.

fig.25 [opposite]
Hubert François Gravelot, *Le Lecteur or The Judicious Lover*, oil on canvas, c. 1745, 311 × 234mm.
Marble Hill House (English Heritage).

The panelling in this interior is painted in a monochrome scheme, with the skirting painted a dark "chocolate" brown. The curtains are paired with a cushion on the window seat.

number of decades. Therefore the likely hypothesis is that the developer George Barnes had the entire interior – except floors and ceilings – of the house (possibly the entire development) painted "lead" colour. The second to fourth layers on the door (which, with the first layer of "lead" colour, covers the period of Handel's occupancy) were a dark chocolate brown, suggesting that subsequent decoration was restricted to specific areas. As was common place in early Georgian interiors, areas which became grubby through use, such as the doors and skirtings, were tidied up by being painted chocolate brown. Using this evidence, a scheme dating from about 1730 (when the chocolate brown was probably first used) has been introduced into the interiors on the first and second floor front and middle rooms, the stairwell and staircase itself. Less chocolate brown has been used on the first floor to give a visual indication of its importance as the principal rooms.

One vital document for the display of the interiors is the inventory which was taken in the August after Handel's death (the contents of which were acquired by Handel's servant John Du Burk) and gives a good indication of the type of furniture and soft furnishings contained within the house (figs. 14 and 26). Although the inventory is not complete (valuable items may have already been given away) it does hold some vital clues. For example, it is probable that Handel ordered his curtains either just prior to or within a few years of moving in, as the 1759 inventory describes a majority of the curtains as "paired" (the only

HANDEL'S HOUSE

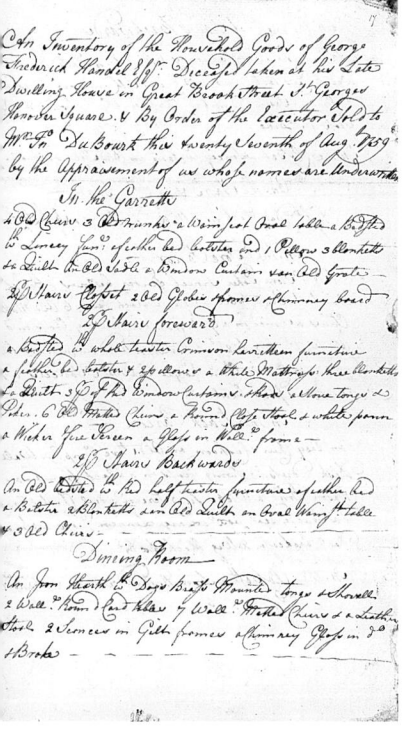

fig.26
An Inventory of the Household Goods of George Frederick Handel Esqr… (first page), manuscript.

British Library (Egerton 3009.E.,ff, 1-18).

The first page of the inventory includes the contents of the garrets, the main bedroom – '2 pr Stairs foreward' – and the front room first floor, described as the 'Dineing Room'.

exception is the ground floor closet which lists 'a Wind^W Curtain'). Paired curtains were the standard curtain design in the 1720s but by the 1750s were extremely unfashionable. In the Georgian period, it was the accepted role of the woman of the house to supervise the updating of domestic interiors and as a busy, unmarried man it is probable that Handel had neither the time nor the inclination to redecorate according to the latest fashions. During the 1730s and 1740s he certainly had more important and pressing issues to occupy him.

The inventory also gives descriptions of fabrics and colour. For example, in accordance with Georgian hierarchy, the first or principal floor had silk curtains (dyed green) as opposed to harateen – a wool fabric, which was one of the main upholstery fabrics during this period – on the ground and second floor. However, the inventory only lists curtains in the back room on the first floor, the lesser of the two entertaining rooms. These curtains, like much of the furniture listed, are described as "old", presenting further evidence of the unfashionable appearance of Handel's interiors by the time of his death. The lack of curtains in the main room of the house – but the presence of curtains in the back room adjoining it – is intriguing. Silk degrades in sunlight and therefore if curtains had existed at one time in the front room they may have been disposed of prior to the inventory being taken. However, there is no reason to suppose that the south facing window in the back room would have received significantly less sunlight than the north facing windows in the front room. A possible explanation – the only hint that the inventory relates to a musician's house – is that curtains were either removed, or were never installed in this room where rehearsals probably took place, for acoustic reasons.

The furniture listed is mainly walnut with some tables described as 'wainscot' (oak). In the main, the remaining furniture was functional, including rush-matted chairs, supper and card tables. None of Handel's furniture has been traced, but the Trust has gathered together furniture which fits the descriptions in the inventory in order to give an idea of how the rooms functioned during Handel's occupancy. The most

fig.27
William Hogarth, *Francis Matthew Shutz in his bed*, oil on canvas, c. 1755-60, 630 × 755 mm.

Norwich Castle Museum.

Beds with testers supported either by foot posts or by chains from the ceiling were very important items of furniture in the early eighteenth century. The cost of the wooden framework of the bed was negligible; it was the textile hangings, or 'furniture' of the bed which was the expensive element. Red was a popular colour for bedrooms, as seen in this painting, where it is used for the paired curtains and bed hangings.

expensive item listed is a full tester (or canopied) bed, dressed in 'Crimson harriteen' (harateen) which was in the front room on the second floor. Textiles were an indication of wealth and status, and such a bed covered entirely in a good quality fabric would have been a luxury. The Trust has been fortunate in being able to borrow a bed of the type described in the inventory. Crimson harateen and silk braid have been specially woven and dyed, and the upholstery, including curtains and valances, are based on the 1730s full tester bed at Hanbury Hall, Worcestershire (National Trust) (fig.28). Following the inventory, the bed linen includes a bolster, pillows, linen sheets, blankets, a quilt and mattresses which have been produced with the assistance of the Historic Royal Palaces.

In 1998 the Handel House Collections Trust acquired the Byrne Collection, a major Handel collection which consists of several hundred

fig.28
Full tester bed, 1730–35, Hanbury Hall, Worcestershire.

The National Trust.

The design of the new hangings is based on this similar style bed, which is still hung with its original woollen damask.

fig.29
Unknown artist, *Margaret [Peg] Woffington*, oil on canvas, c.1758, 902 × 1067mm.

National Portrait Gallery, London.

The inventory also lists the various items of bedding: 'a feather bed bolster & 2 pillows a White Mattress three blankets & a Quilt'. Beds of this period frequently had two or sometimes three mattresses, covered with a stout linen or a ticking, placed on a bed base usually made up of timber planks of various widths, or a mesh of stretched cords. The base mattress would have been quite solid, stuffed with horsehair and/or wool, and the top mattress would have had a feather filling. Handel enjoyed his comfort and he is likely to have had good quality linen sheets and linen covers for the bolster and two pillows. The quilt was probably made of white silk with a wool wadding centre, and hand stitched in a simple diamond pattern as shown in this contemporary painting.

HANDEL HOUSE MUSEUM COMPANION

fig.30
W A Mozart's arrangement for string quartet of a keyboard fugue originally composed by Handel c.1717. First page of Mozart's autograph written in Vienna c.1782–3.

The Byrne Collection,
Handel House Collections Trust.

fig.31
[Rev.] John Mainwaring, *Memoirs of the Life of the Late George Frederic Handel…*, printed book with marginalia by Charles Jennens, pub. Robert and James Dodsley, 1760, London, p.152,.

The Byrne Collection,
Handel House Collections Trust.

In the margin next to *Semele*, Jennens has written, 'No oratorio but a bawdy opera'.

objects, including a letter from Handel to Charles Jennens regarding *Belshazzar* and *Messiah*, an autograph leaf from *Esther*, Mozart's autograph arrangement of a Handel fugue (fig.30), John Mainwaring's *Memoirs of the life of the late George Frederic Handel* (1760) annotated by Jennens (fig.31 and fig.67, p.77), early editions of operas and oratorios, and prints, portraits and sculpture. In 1996 and 1998 respectively the Collections Trust also acquired two important oil paintings; a portrait of one of Handel's opera sopranos Faustina Bordoni (?1700–81) by Bartolomeo Nazari (1699–1758) (fig.56, p.66) and a portrait of Jennens by Thomas Hudson (1701–79) (fig.69, p.80). A selection, including both portraits, has been integrated into the fine art displays in No. 25 Brook Street and a further selection from the manuscripts and printed scores are displayed in No. 23 Brook Street.

The interiors of No. 25 Brook Street as they are now presented are a scholarly re-creation, using all available documentation, prototypes and archaeological evidence. As such they are as close as we are ever likely to get to the interiors that Handel would have known.

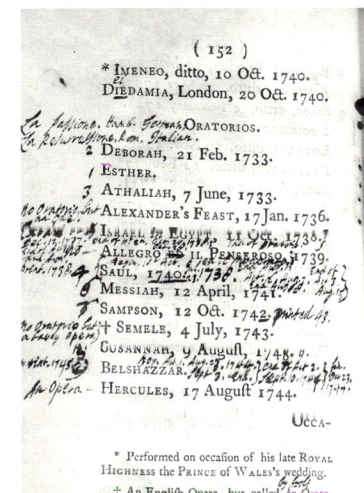

3

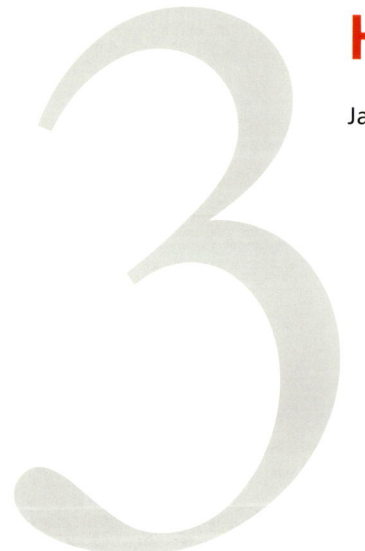

Handel's London

Jacqueline Riding

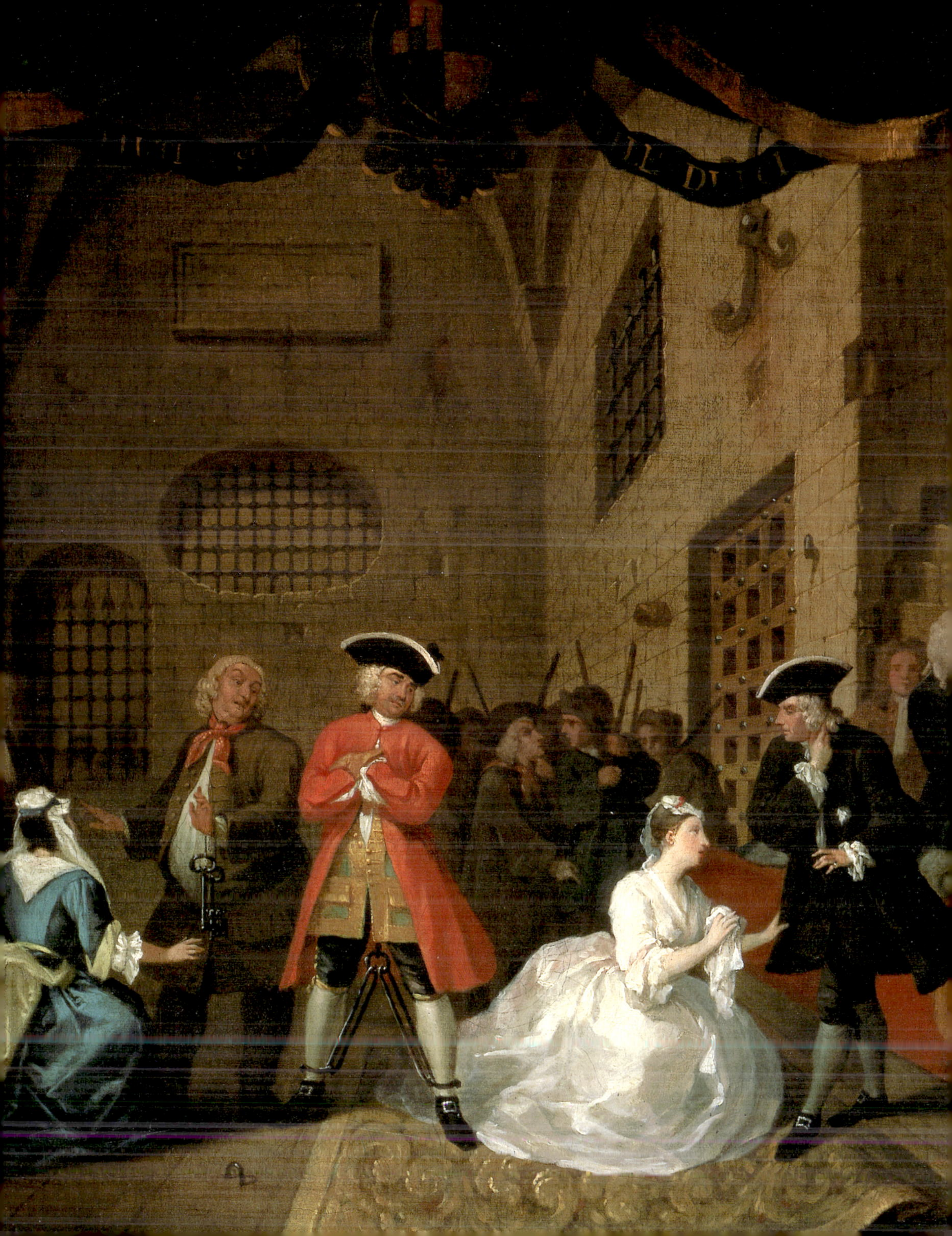

[previous page]
Detail of fig 32

fig.32
William Hogarth, *A Scene from 'The Beggar's Opera' VI*, oil on canvas, 1731, 572 × 762mm.

Tate Collections.

> In these times, whoever wishes to be eminent in music goes to England. In Italy and France there is something to be heard and learned; in England something to be earned'.
>
> Johann Mattheson *Das neu-eröffnete Orchestra*, Hamburg 1713

For those with entrepreneurial spirit, Britain and in particular London, offered opportunities rarely found in comparable countries and cities in mainland Europe. As Mattheson's comment suggests, the perception amongst European composers and musicians was that in England, such musical adventurers could not only be "eminent" but that there was serious money to made. That his friend should have such an opinion offers potential incite into Handel's own motivation. Mattheson's perception is borne out by the great numbers of musicians (and indeed on a broader scale artists and artisans) from the continent who came to try their luck in Britain. Some, like the French Huguenots, came because of religious persecution in their native land, but for many it was the appeal of a relatively free market, which contrasted so dramatically with the bondage of continental church or court patronage. Aside from Handel himself, one of the most significant was the Italian composer Bononcini, who arrived in 1720 at the instigation of Lord Burlington, initially providing operas for the Royal Academy and leaving after a scandal involving plagiarism in 1732. Of the many foreign musicians who are known to have worked in Britain during this period some, like Handel, became major contributors to the musical and social life of their adopted country, and remained until their deaths. These include the German composers John Christopher Pepusch (1667–1752) (fig.35) and John Ernest Galliard (c.1687–1749), the Italian cellist Nicola Francesco Haym (1678–1729) and his compatriots, the composer Attilio Ariosti (1666–1729?), the composer and violinist Francesco Geminiani (1687–1762) as well as Handel's copyist J C Smith the elder and his son. As an example of their integration into London's musical scene, a majority of the aforementioned were either founders or subsequent members of the Academy of Vocal [later Ancient] Music (founded 1726).

Throughout the eighteenth century, London (the cities of London and Westminster) was the place to be for anyone – native or foreign – who had any ambition. Through trade and colonial expansion, London was the centre of an increasingly buoyant national economy. It was where the royal family lived for most of the year – and thus the court – and was the centre of government and Parliament. By 1750, London held over one fifth of the total population of Britain and was at least ten times bigger than the largest of provincial towns. It was the national centre of fashion and patronage, of luxury production and consumption. It provided the greatest access to cultural information from abroad, was the hub of a growing press network as well as printing and publishing.

By the death of Queen Anne the court was no longer the centre of the nation's political and social life; this role had been assumed by the proliferation of gentlemen's clubs, coffee houses (of which there were over two thousand by 1750) and theatres, most of which were located

fig.33
Alexander Van Aken after Thomas Hudson, *John Christopher Pepusch*, mezzotint engraving, c.1735, 310 × 253mm.
Private Collection.

in London's West End. From the last quarter of the seventeenth century, London could boast a number of public venues where musical entertainments were available – instigated by music-loving amateurs and entrepreneurs – such as the York Buildings in Villiers Street and 'Mr Hickford's Great Room' located near to the King's Theatre. It is not known whether Handel ever performed at these venues, but he is believed to have played at one of London's most unusual; the room above Thomas Britton's coal shop in Clerkenwell. From 1678 to his death in 1714, Britton (fig.34) held concerts here, which, according to one observer, was 'the weekly resort of the old, the young, the gay and the fair of all ranks, including the highest order of nobility.' As a venue renowned for the status of its audience as well as its novelty value, it is likely that Handel would have attended at least one or more of these gatherings in the company of one of his early London contacts, among whom the poet John Hughes (1677–1720) was a regular participant. Pepusch and Galliard are also known to have performed there.

But more important to Handel's early career in London was the recent introduction of Italian opera. The Queen's (later King's) Theatre, designed and managed by the architect and playwright Sir John Vanburgh, opened in 1705 and under a succession of managers, Owen MacSwinny (d.1754), Aaron Hill (1685–1750) and John James Heidegger continued as the focus for Italian opera until the 1730s. One of London's more colourful musical personalities, MacSwinny (fig.35) is best remembered for absconding with the takings for Handel's third opera *Teseo* in January 1713, although during his exile on the continent, he continued to be useful to Handel and the Royal Academy by acting as a scout for singers. Despite a short period as manager, it was under the aegis of Aaron Hill that Handel's *Rinaldo* was commissioned and performed. From 1713 the management passed to Heidegger with whom Handel maintained a close working relationship at the King's Theatre until the advent of the Opera of the Nobility. In addition to opera, Heidegger also organised masquerades, which proved very lucrative, if not overly popular with the Bishop of London. Aside from theatres, by the latter part of the century London had approximately sixty pleasure gardens, the most famous of which were at Vauxhall (established 1732) and Ranelagh (established 1742) all of which provided further outlets for music composition and performance.

 Music and theatre, as with all areas of London life, was highly politicised. After the Act of Settlement in 1701 there was a genuine fear that a Catholic monarchy might be re-established through force by the dispossessed heirs of King James II (deposed 1688). The succession upon the death of Queen Anne was therefore a highly contested political and religious issue. Georg Ludwig, Elector of Hanover succeeded to the British throne – by-passing over fifty individuals with closer family ties to Queen Anne – solely because he was a Protestant and they were not. It should also be remembered that the concept of "Britain" and "Britons" was a very recent political construct (the Act of Union between England, Wales and Scotland having been signed in 1707). With intermittent conflict throughout the century with foreign Catholic powers – in particular France, who persistently backed the Jacobite cause – it seemed that Britons were in an on-going struggle for national sovereignty. Such sensitivity to "foreign invasion" also affected British reception to foreign culture: in the 1720s, for example, "Catholic plots" were discussed in the same breath as Italian opera. When Handel returned to London in 1712 these political tensions would soon be at

fig.34
John Wollaston, *Thomas Britton*,
oil on canvas, 1703, 743 × 622mm.
National Portrait Gallery, London.

fig.35
After Peter Van Bleeck, *Owen MacSwinny*,
oil on canvas, 1737, 768 × 638mm.
National Portrait Gallery, London.

their peak. As historians have observed, given that music, and in particular opera – the most significant of the performing genres in Europe – was inextricably linked with the political elite, it is not surprising that Handel seems to have been used by the Hanoverians as their cultural trail blazer.

Athough *émigrés* from Roman Catholic countries risked hostility from the predominantly Protestant population, they had nothing to fear from British patrons who decidedly favoured Continental art, architecture or music. Alive or dead, French or Italian, a foreign artist or musician was more lauded and more sought after than his living British counterpart. This bias was the result of extensive travel abroad (above all in Italy) by wealthy young men via the so-called "Grand Tour"; a cultural institution both Chandos and Burlington had undertaken. Each year Grand Tourists returned to Britain in their thousands, dressed in the latest Parisian fashions, weighed down by "Old Masters" and antiquities, the sound of Italian opera still ringing in their ears, convinced of the innate superiority of Continental culture.

Undoubtedly a large proportion of European artists and musicians – Handel included – came to England in order to exploit the prejudice of the social elite. But despite this seemingly hopeless situation for native musicians and composers there was a strong and vociferous group within literary and artistic circles who championed the setting of English texts to music – thereby continuing (or perhaps reviving) the native musical tradition which had been dealt so cruel a blow by the early death of Henry Purcell (1659–1695). In 1732, Aaron Hill made an impassioned plea to Handel 'to deliver us from our *Italian bondage*; and demonstrate, that *English* is soft enough for Opera, when compos'd by poets, who know how to distinguish the *sweetness* of our tongue, from the *strength* of it, where the last is necessary.' Perhaps the most influential advocate was the poet Alexander Pope (1688–1744) (fig.36) whom Handel met either at Burlington House or Cannons (Pope may have been involved with the text for the original version of *Esther*). In *The Dunciad* (published 1729) Pope celebrated the extraordinary success of the English ballad-opera, *The Beggar's Opera* (fig.32, p.38), first performed in January 1728, which 'drove out of England the Italian Opera, which carry'd all before it for ten years.' *The Beggar's Opera* was the brainchild of another of Handel's early contacts, John Gay (1685–1732) who, with John Hughes and possibly Pope, provided the text for *Acis and Galatea,* which Gay described as an 'English Pastoral Opera'. *The Beggar's Opera* was first performed at the Lincoln's Inn Theatre under the aegis of John Rich, with Gay as librettist and the orchestration and overture provided by Pepusch. Highly satirical and unashamedly English, it cheerfully turned *opera seria* on its head, making heroes of highwaymen and villains of state officials, mixing the tunes of popular ballads with Italian-style music – some of which were Handel's own – and replacing recitative with spoken English. Nothing was sacred, be it Italian opera or the government of the day. Thus the love-triangle between the highwayman, Captain Macheath, Polly Peachum and Lucy Lockit was as much a send-up of Handel and his two warring sopranos, Cuzzoni and Faustina, as it was of the prime minister Sir Robert Walpole (1676–1745), his wife and mistress. Its success highlighted a gap in the market and although it did not cause the downfall of Italian opera, it was an indication of a change in taste. This change was perhaps inevitable. As Leslie Orrery writes, '*Opera seria* required for its fullest flowering the ambience of a rich, self-centred autocratic court, with

fig.36
Studio of **Michael Dahl**, *Alexander Pope*, oil on canvas, c.1727, 762 × 635mm,
National Portrait Gallery, London.

HANDEL'S LONDON

fig.37
William Hogarth, *The Enraged Musician*, etching & engraving, 1741, 332 × 405mm.
Tate Collections.

fig.38 [opposite]
William Hogarth, *The painter and his pug*, oil on canvas, 1745, 900 × 699mm.
Tate Collections.

fig.39
After **Francesco Bartolozzi**, *Dr Thomas Arne*, engraving, pub. 1782, 215 × 160mm.
Private Collection.

a ruler vain or insecure enough to welcome sycophantic flattery. This partly explains Handel's difficulties in London, where *opera seria* was offered, not to a self-admiring court but to a public that had already moved on to the next stage of political awareness.'

The visual arts also provided a powerful forum for criticism and satire. In his print *The Taste of the Town, or Masquerades and Operas* (published 1724), the self-proclaimed 'Britophil' William Hogarth (fig.38) lampooned what he perceived as the bad taste of a public who preferred foreign culture over the native literary and theatrical masterpieces of Congreve, Milton, Dryden and Shakespeare. Unsurprisingly, *The Beggar's Opera* had inspired no less than six canvasses and in *The Enraged Musician* (1741) (fig.37) Hogarth depicted the victory of native culture – represented by the everyday hurly-burly of a London street – over foreign culture, personified by the Italian-looking violinist, whose music-making is disturbed by the noise outside his own window. *The Beggar's Opera* is triumphantly advertised on the left-hand wall.

Handel too must have sensed this change. He doggedly continued with Italian opera throughout the 1730s but responded to the general mood by introducing English oratorio and oratorio-type works into his programme. Any lingering doubt appears to have been finally resolved during the highly successful Dublin visit. On Handel's return, the production of music set to English text continued and developed in earnest. Handel quickly achieved an unrivalled position which few of his contemporaries even attempted to challenge. In the main, Handel's contemporaries appear to have accepted his superiority with good grace. One obvious exception was Thomas Arne (1710–78) (fig.39) the composer of the patriotic masque, *Alfred* (1740) with its rousing finale, *Rule, Britannia!*. Sir John Hawkins described Arne as having 'always

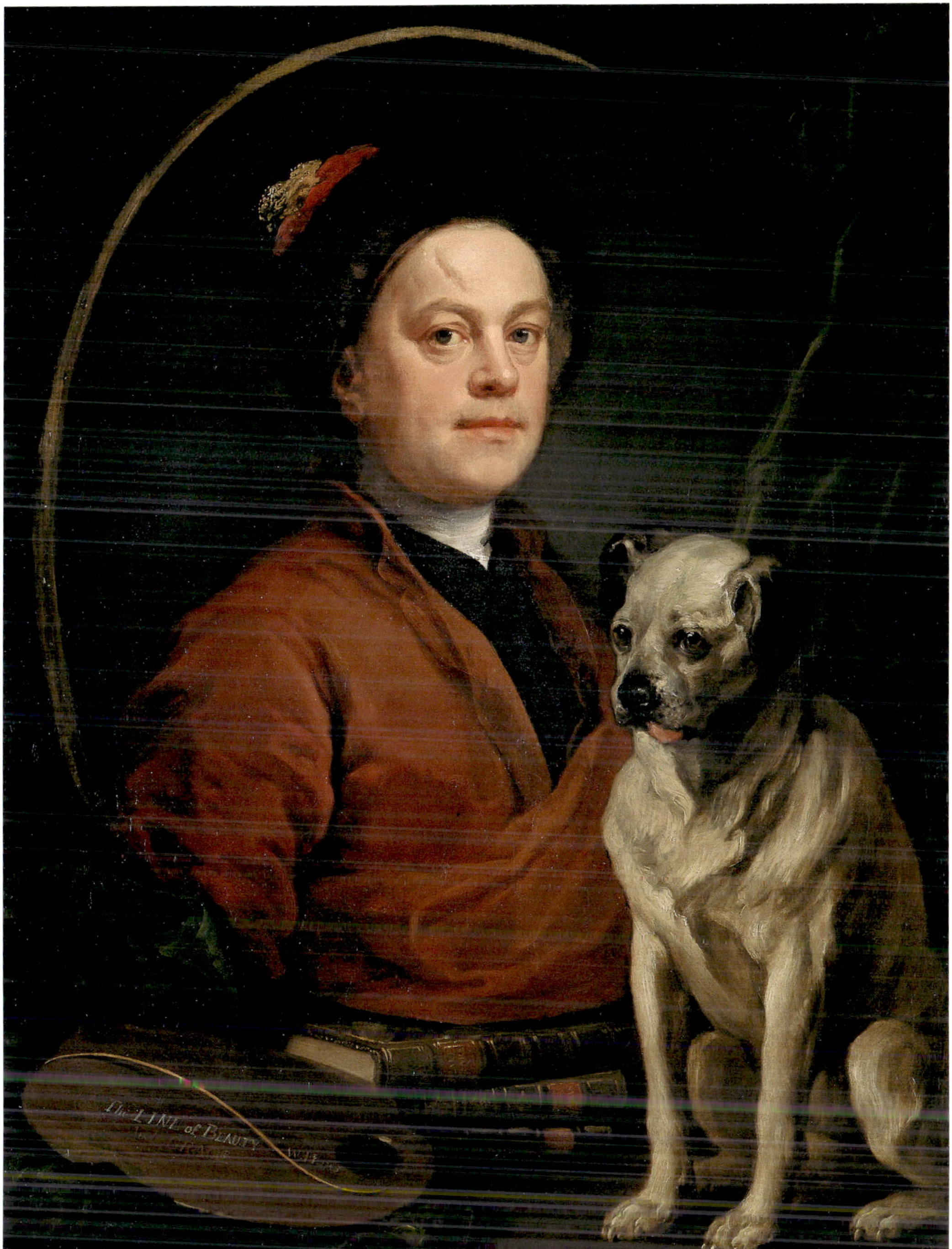
The LINE of BEAUTY

HANDEL'S LONDON

fig.40
Unknown engraver, *Perspective of the Magnificent Building erected in Green Park for the Royal Fire Works...*, engraving, pub. 1749, 230 × 390mm.

Handel House Collections Trust.

regarded Handel as a tyrant and usurper, against whom he frequently rebelled'– but to no avail. Alexander Pope – a critic in 1729 – now celebrated Handel in *The New Dunciad* (published March 1742) as the prime mover against Italian opera.

Handel's focus on music set to English text appears to have encouraged a change in the general perception of the composer himself. He had been a British citizen since 1727, but as Pope's *volte face* suggests, Handel's wholehearted engagement with the English language – the setting of texts by Milton, Dryden, Congreve and collaboration with the librettists James Harris (1709–80), Charles Jennens, Newburgh Hamilton and Thomas Morell – eased his acceptance as "one of us". Certainly his *Judas Maccabaeus* (performed 1747) was a well-timed and conscious engagement

A Perspective View of Vaux Hall Garden

John Maurer, *A Perspective View of Vaux Hall Garden*, etching, pub. 1744, 235 × 407mm.
London Borough of Lambeth Archives.

This print shows the original location of Roubiliac's statue (far right). The building to the left housed the orchestra and organ.

with the upsurge of British patriotism during the second Jacobite rebellion.

As Donald Burrows has pointed out, the rehearsal and performance of Handel's *Fireworks Music* in April 1749, (fig.40) followed by his annual performances at and on behalf of the Foundling Hospital contributed to his celebrity status amongst a much broader British public. Newspapers reported an audience of 12,000 people for the rehearsal of the *Fireworks Music* alone. Although he composed very little specifically for performance at London's numerous pleasure gardens, Handel's music was regularly played at these highly fashionable venues. Since 1738, Handel had been the presiding genius at the most famous of these at Vauxhall when Louis François Roubiliac's celebrated statue of the composer as a raffish Apollo was installed (fig.41). If this sculpture served as a fitting monument to Handel's unique status in London during his lifetime, his burial and monument in Westminster Abbey represented his posthumous status as a national cultural great.

Handel The Man

Jacqueline Riding

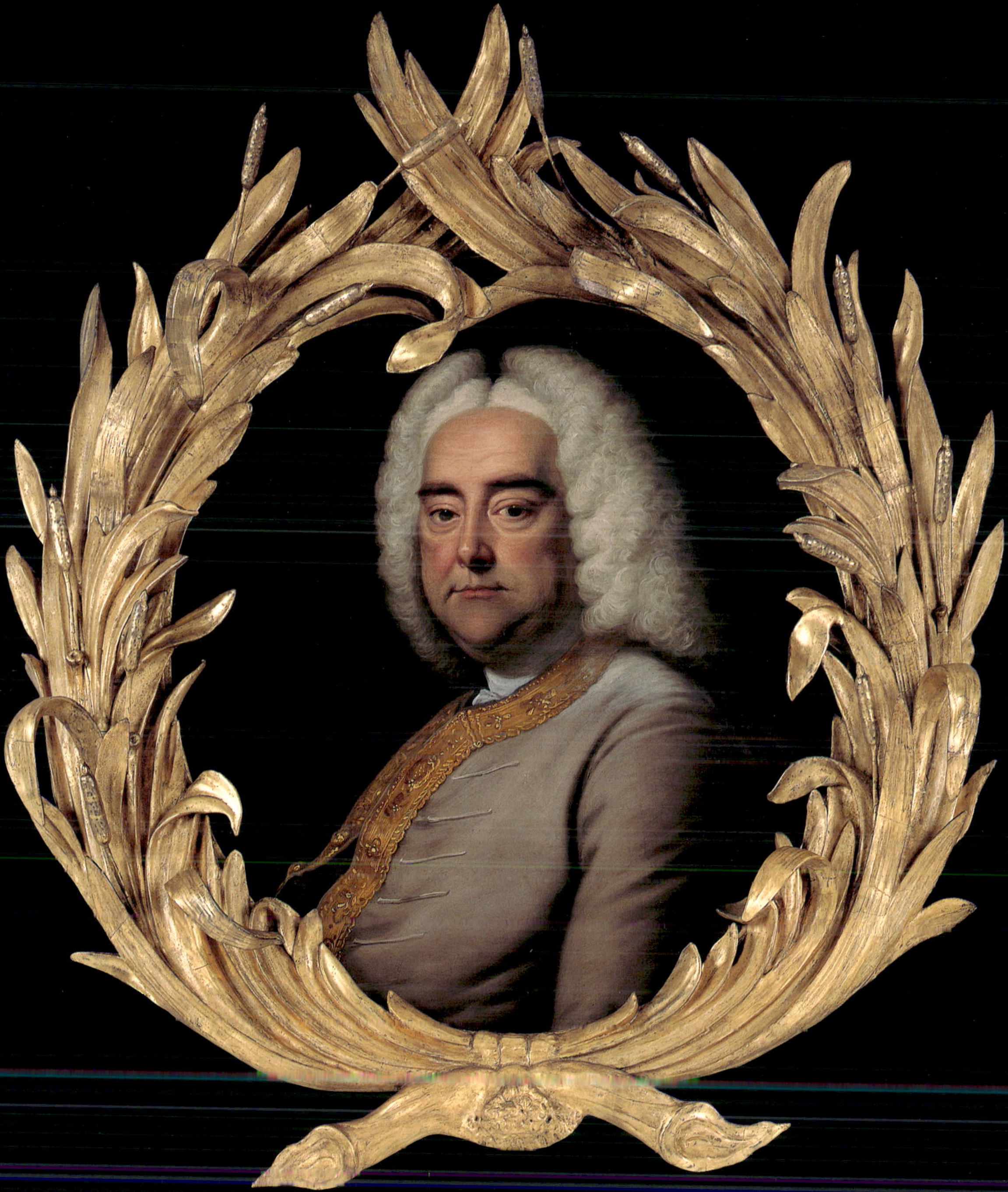

fig.42 [previous page]
After **Thomas Hudson**, *G F Handel*,
oil on canvas.

The Royal Collection.

This portrait is a copy after the portrait by Hudson dated 1756 (National Potrait Gallery, London).

fig.43
Francesco Bartolozzi after Sir Joshua Reynolds,
Dr Charles Burney, stipple engraving, pub. 1784, 226 × 177mm.

Private Collection.

fig.44 [opposite]
Unknown artist, *A Musician*, believed to be Handel, oil on copper, 1713, 126 × 97mm.

The Byrne Collection,
Handel House Collections Trust.

'It was thought better to leave the Reader to collect his character from the LIFE itself, than to attempt the drawing of it in form.'

John Mainwaring

ALTHOUGH HANDEL'S PUBLIC and professional life is well documented, the man himself, his personality, opinions on non-musical issues and particularly his private life, remain elusive. Handel left to posterity very few letters, no autobiography or diary. Faced with a paucity of intimate detail, Handel's early English biographers, John Mainwaring (c.1724–1807), Dr Charles Burney (1726–1814) (fig.43), Sir John Hawkins (1719–89) and William Coxe (1747–1828) relied upon personal experience of Handel's character in his later years and anecdotes – both flattering and unflattering to the composer's memory – most of which came to light after his death and were no doubt embellished in the telling. Two explanations can be offered; Handel was not only an extraordinarily private individual, but he was clearly very successful at maintaining his privacy. However, in writing about Handel the man, his early biographers cannot be dismissed, for within their writings are certain elements regarding his personality and private life upon which they all agree, and whether the anecdotes are embellished or not there must be at least a grain of truth within them.

Few early portraits survive, but Johann Mattheson, Handel's friend, compatriot and adversary in the famous duel in Hamburg, offers the following brief description; 'Handel at the time of the quarrel, was twenty years of age; tall, strong, broad-shouldered, and muscular, consequently well able to defend himself'. During his years in Italy, Mainwaring writes that the young Handel's 'youth and comliness', coupled with his fame and musical ability, was sufficient to capture the amorous attentions of the Italian soprano, Vittoria Tarquini. Later, in Hanover, the Dowager Electress described him as 'quite a handsome man'. His appearance from middle age to just prior to his death can be traced through the portraits of Philip Mercier (fig.65, p.75), Thomas Hudson (figs.42 and 45) and perhaps most revealingly, the sculptures of

Louis François Roubiliac (1702/5–62). Roubiliac produced a number of sculptures of the composer during his lifetime (including the full-length commissioned for Vauxhall Pleasure Gardens) (fig.46) and took a mould of Handel's face soon after the composer's death, from which casts were produced. It was also Roubiliac who sculpted Handel's monument in Westminster Abbey (fig.9, p.19). In both oil and marble, Handel appears as a man of great dignity, presence and determination. The oil portraits reveal that he had distinctively pale blue eyes and dark, full eyebrows. From his middle years, Handel appears to have been of heavy stature as Burney writes, 'The figure of HANDEL was large, and he was somewhat corpulent, and unwieldy in his motions'. However, in support of the artists' brush and chisel, he continues 'his countenance…was full of fire and dignity; and such as impressed ideas of superiority and genius.'

His corpulence in later years can be attributed to – as Coxe charmingly phrases it – 'a culpable indulgence in the sensual gratifications of the table.' Early in his career, Handel may have acquired a taste for the culinary high life through his association with princes, cardinals and aristocrats. To his middle-class biographers, however, it was an indulgence which they found difficult to come to terms with. Mainwaring wrote, 'He certainly paid more attention to it, than is becoming in any man' but attempts to justify it through Handel's 'incessant and intense application to the studies of his profession. This rendered constant and large supplies of nourishment the more necessary to recruit his exhausted spirits.' Aside from this, his only documented indulgence was art collecting and by his death he had amassed a sizable collection of pre-dominantly seventeenth-century Old Masters (see chapter 2).

There exist two anecdotes which refer to Handel reserving his finer food and drink for his own secret consumption whilst entertaining friends in his house. The occasion involving the artist Joseph Goupy (c.1680–c.1770) a scene designer for the Royal Academy and until this point an intimate friend of the composer, resulted, as legend has it, in the production of a scurrilous caricature depicting Handel as a pig (fig.47), which was engraved and copied for general circulation – surely too extreme a reaction under the circumstances.

Contrasted with this alleged lack of generosity is Handel's loyalty and charity. As the only son of a late second marriage, Handel was acutely aware of his responsibilities toward his widowed mother – Dorothea Elizabeth (1651–1730), widowed in 1697 – and direct family (as his will reveals), even though his visits to Halle were rare after settling in London. His niece Johanne Frederike Flörcke (1711–71), the married daughter of Handel's sister Dorothea Sophie (1687–1718) and Michael Dietrich Michaelsen (1680–1748) (fig.48) (Handel regularly corresponded with the latter) was the main beneficiary of the composer's will. In addition, Handel financially assisted the widow of Zachow, his teacher in Halle, through which we can glean a sense of loyalty, respect and gratitude to his former master. The greatest examples of

fig.45 [above]
John Faber after Thomas Hudson, *Handel*, mezzotint engraving, 1749, 359 × 254mm.
Private Collection.

fig.46
Louis François Roubiliac, *Handel*, the Vauxhall Gardens statue, marble, 1737–8.
Victoria and Albert Museum.

fig.47 [opposite]
Unknown engraver after Joseph Goupy, *The Charming Brute*, engraving, 1754, 302 × 235mm.
Gerald Coke Handel Collection.
Photograph, National Portrait Gallery, London.

The Figure's odd — yet who would think?
(Within this Tunn of Meat & Drink)
There dwells the Soul of soft Desires,
And all that HARMONY inspires:

THE
Charming
BRUTE

Can Contrast such as this be found?
Upon the Globe's extensive Round:
There can — you Hogshead is his Seat,
His sole Devotion is — to Eat.

Pub. according to Act of Parliam.t March 21 1754

fig.48
Johann Christoph Sysang after
Christian Heinrich Sporleder,
Michael Dietrich Michaelsen, engraving, n.d.,
308 × 194 mm.

Gerald Coke Handel Collection.
Photograph, National Portrait Gallery, London.

Handel's charitable spirit are his associations with the 'Fund for the Support of Decay'd Musicians' (now the Royal Society of Musicians) and the Foundling Hospital (founded 1738 and 1739 respectively). Handel was a founding member of the former, conducting benefit performances gratis and donating the ticket sales. Further, the charity received £1,000 in Handel's will. The Foundling Hospital (fig.49) was the first institution in England dedicated to the care of abandoned children and the benefit concerts conducted by the composer drew huge crowds to the hospital. Burney calculated that between 1749 and 1759, the hospital received £10,299 through Handel's direct influence. Handel, who became a governor of the hospital, also donated the Chapel organ, composed the hospital's "anthem" and gave to the hospital a fair copy of *Messiah*, which remains one of the charity's greatest treasures.

Indications of Handel's independent and determined spirit are evident from his childhood. Handel pursued his love of music against the wishes of his fatherGeorg Friedrich (1622–97) and during his time in both Germany and Italy avoided any court position that restricted his freedom. In London, despite his connection with the Hanoverian Court, Handel maintained a control over his career unequalled by his contemporaries. Mainwaring expands this independence to explain his life-long bachelor state; 'In the sequel of his life he refused the highest offers from persons of the greatest distinction; nay, the highest favours from the fairer of the sex, only because he would not be cramped or confined by particular attachments.' Handel's sexual orientation has enjoyed some interest in recent years. Within Hawkins's statement, 'His social affections were not very strong; and to this it may be imputed that he spent his whole life in a state of celibacy; that he had no female attachment of another kind may be ascribed to a better reason', the "better reason" has been interpreted as homosexuality. A more likely interpretation of Hawkins's meaning, is that the unmarried Handel did not have <u>any</u> intimate relations with women because of his scrupulous morals. Whether he was a homosexual remains speculation.

Handel maintained a small and discrete circle of friends, supporters and collaborators. The composer Georg Philipp Telemann was a lifelong friend from their student years and in 1754 it is recorded that Handel sent his old friend a crate of exotic plants. In London his closest associates included J C Smith elder and younger (the former Handel's principal copyist and the latter Handel's pupil during 1720s and 1730s, becoming the aging composer's amanuensis during the 1750s), Dr Thomas Morell (1703–84) (librettist for *Judas Maccabaeus*, *Theodora* and *Jephtha*), the brothers James, Thomas and George Harris, their cousin Anthony Ashley Cooper, 4th Earl of Shaftesbury (1711–71), Mrs Mary Pendarves (1700–88) (later Mrs Delany) and her brother Bernard Granville. His near neighbour in Upper Brook Street, Mrs Pendarves recalled an intimate *soirée* at her home, attended by her brother and Shaftesbury, where 'Mr Handel was in the best humour in the world, and played lessons and accompanied Strada [the soprano Anna Maria Strada del Pò] and all the ladies that sung from seven o' the clock till eleven.'

Handel's explosive temper, which was often accompanied by colourful language, appears to have been well-known and generally humoured by his contemporaries. Equally, Handel's rather dry sense of humour is

fig.49
Charles Grignion and Pierre-Charles Canot after Samuel Wale, *A Perspective View of the Foundling Hospital, with Emblematic Figures*, engraving, 1749, 292 × 429mm.
Guildhall Library.

referred to in several instances, offering a rare lighter side to his character. Mattheson recalled that 'he used to be very arch, for he had always a dry way of making the gravest people laugh, without laughing himself': an attribute which was observed in later life. Burney recounts, in a performance in Dublin, that the violinist and orchestra leader, Matthew Dubourg lost his way during a solo improvisation 'but at length, coming to the shake, which was to terminate this long close, HANDEL, to the great delight of the audience, and augmentation of applause, cried out loud enough to be heard in the most remote parts of the theatre: "You are welcome home, Mr Dubourg!" With reference to the various languages which Handel spoke, Dr W C Quinn in a letter to Burney dated 1788 recalled, 'I had the pleasure of seeing and conversing with Mr Handel, who, with his other excellences, was possessed of a great stock of humour. No man ever told a story with more effect. But it was requisite for the hearer to have a competent knowledge of at least four languages – English, French, Italian, and German, for in his narrative he made use of them.'

During the last decade of his life, Handel suffered from failing eyesight, culminating in full blindness by 1754. During the composition of *Jephtha*, Handel noted in German in the margin, 'got as far as this on Wednesday 13 February 1751, unable to continue because the sight of my left eye is so weakened.' Attempts were made to restore his sight – including recourse to the 'quack' oculist John Taylor (1702–72) who had operated on Johann Sebastian Bach (1685–1750) with failure in 1751 – but the operations were in Mainwaring's words 'as fruitless as they were painful.' For his friends and biographers this situation was to cast Handel in a tragic light. Burney writes that Handel 'was always much disturbed and agitated by the similar circumstances of *Samson*, whenever the affecting air in that Oratorio of "Total Eclipse, no Sun, no Moon," &c. was performed.' The 1759 inventory of Handel's Brook Street house, lists a half-tester bed in the room adjoining Handel's bedroom, which was probably used by a man-servant as Handel required greater assistance due to his blindness. The imposing full-length portrait commissioned by Charles Jennens and now in the National Portrait Gallery, dates from this period (1756).

Handel had been born into the Lutheran faith; after settling in Brook Street he may have begun attending services at his local parish church of St George's, Hanover Square (fig.50). Certainly towards the end of his life, when his deteriorating eyesight seems to have increased his religious fervour, Handel became a regular attender, as Hawkins writes;

For the last two or three years of his life he was used to attend divine service in his own parish church of St. George's, Hanover-square, where, during prayers, the eyes that at this instant are employed in a faint portrait of his excellencies, have seen him on his knees, expressing by his looks and gesticulations the utmost fervour of devotion.

fig.50
Unknown engraver, *A View of St Georges Church Hanover Square*, engraving, pub. 1751, 246 × 402mm.
Guildhall Library.

HANDEL THE MAN

fig.51 [opposite]
Cast of the death(?)-mask taken by Louis François Roubiliac, plaster.
Photograph, National Portrait Gallery, London.

Handel died at his Brook Street house on 14 April 1759. James Smyth, a perfumer in nearby Bond Street, wrote in a letter to Bernard Granville dated 17 April 1759;

According to your request to me when you left London, that I would let you know when our good friend departed this life, on Saturday last at 8 o'clock in the morn died the great and good Mr.Handel. He was sensible to the last moment; made a codicil to his will on Tuesday, ordered to be buried privately at Westminster Abbey, and a monument not to exceed £600 for him…He took leave of all his friends on Friday morning, and desired to see nobody but the Doctor and Apothecary and myself. At 7 o'clock in the evening he took leave of me, and told me we "should meet again"; as soon as I was gone he told his servant "not to let me come to him any more, for that he had now done with the world". He died as he lived – a good Christian, with a true sense of his duty to God and man, and in perfect charity with all the world.

If the serenity of his last hours as described by Smyth is correct, Handel probably retired to his bedroom on the Friday evening (incidentally Good Friday) and died peacefully in his bed the following morning. The *Whitehall Evening Post* on 14 April reported, 'When he went home from the Messiah Yesterday Se'nnight, he took to his Bed, and has never rose from it since.' Immediately the tributes began. In the newspapers, Handel was described as 'deservedly celebrated' and 'that eminent Master of Musick' and valedictory poems were published. Mainwaring's biography was published the year after Handel's death and is important as the first single volume biography of a composer. Similarly, Dr Samuel Arnold (1740–1802) published his edition of Handel's works between 1787 and 1797, which was the first attempt at a collected edition of the works of any composer. In 1784 the great Handel Commemoration, a series of concerts held at Westminster Abbey and the Pantheon in Oxford Street (for which Burney wrote an illustrated account, published 1785) was testament to the extraordinary standing of the composer and his music within decades of his death. As Burney writes, 'it will be difficult to find, either in ancient or modern

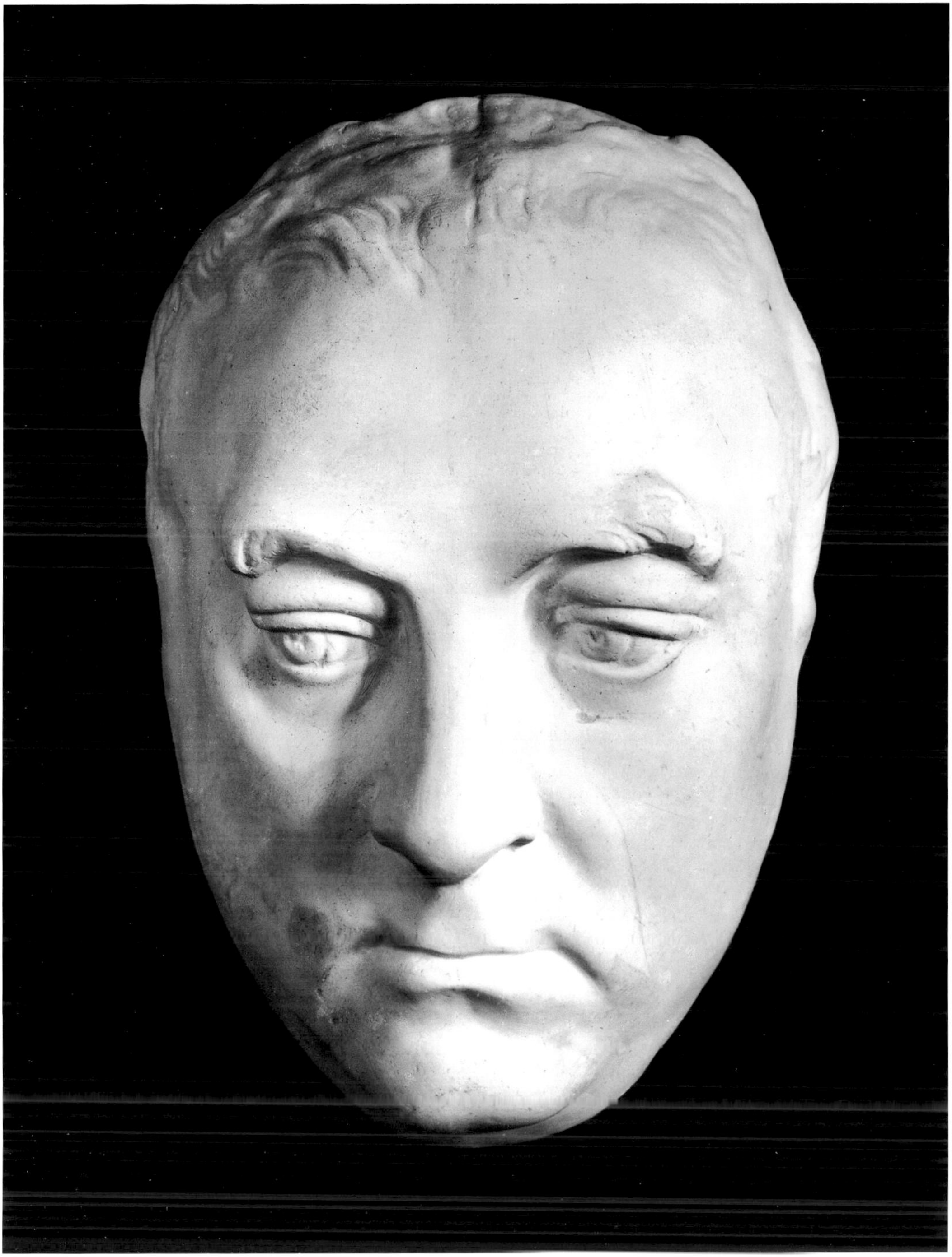

60

fig.52 [opposite]
James Heath after Biagio Rebecca. *Apotheosis of Handel*, engraving, pub. 1787, 320 × 222mm.

The Byrne Collection,
Handel House Collections Trust.

fig.53
J Collyer after E F Burney, *View of the Orchestra and Performers in Westminster Abbey, during the Commemoration of Handel*, engraving, 1785, 232 × 165mm.

Private Collection.

history, a more liberal and splendid example of gratitude to a deceased artist, in any other country.' His posthumous status was assisted by the enthusiasm of King George III: as Handel himself said, 'While that boy lives, my music will never want a protector.'

Handel emerges as a man of contrasts: irascible and selfish but in greater measure, amusing, kind-hearted and benevolent. However, Handel's most overriding trait was his single-minded dedication to his music coupled with a powerful self-belief which enabled him to survive the turbulent periods that littered his London career.

5

Rehearsal and Performance

Jacqueline Riding

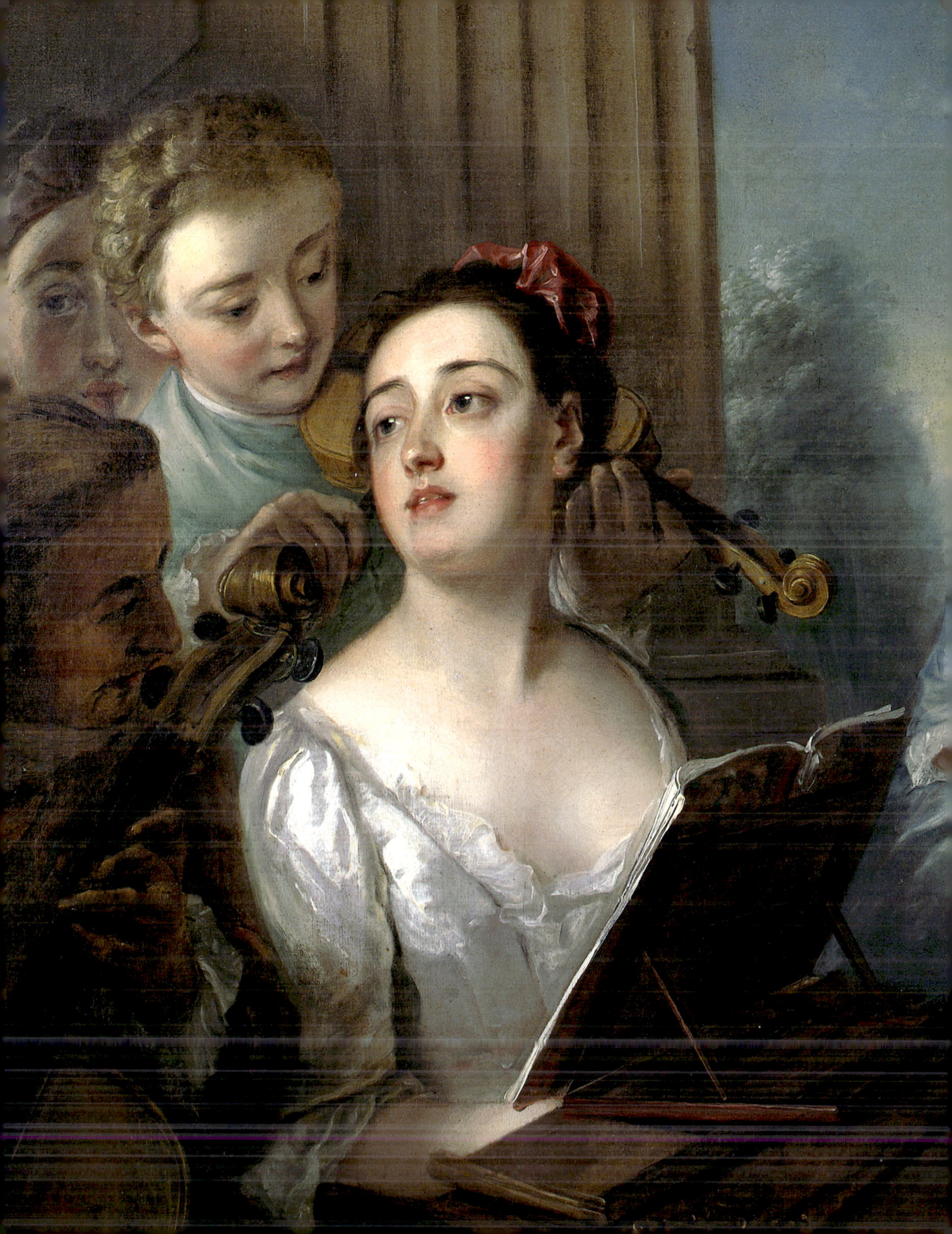

[previous page]
Detail of fig.54

REHEARSAL AND PERFORMANCE

fig.54
Philip Mercier, *A Music Party*, oil on canvas,
c.1737–40,
1026 × 1270mm.

Tate Collections.

THE PROCESS TOWARDS a performance probably involved initial individual rehearsals for soloists and lead instrumentalists, and later full rehearsals at the performance venue. The full rehearsals, particularly for opera, were "public" (in that they were attended by ticket holders) although they were not advertised. Opera subscribers would have considered such access their privilege. The smaller rehearsals may have occurred at the venue itself, to one side of the theatre during a general rehearsal, or in a smaller room in the vicinity. From a variety of sources, it is evident that rehearsals with Handel could be stormy affairs, particularly if his soloists had the audacity to challenge his judgment. The most famous example involved the newly arrived Italian diva, Francesa Cuzzoni (c.1700–70), during rehearsals of *Ottone* (1722/1723) probably held at the King's Theatre:

> Having one day some words with CUZZONI on her refusing to sing *Falsa imagine* in OTTONE; Oh! Madame (said he) je scais bien que Vous êtes une veritable Diablesse: mais je Vous ferai savoir, moi, que je suis Beelzebub le *Chèf* des Diables.†
> With this he took her up by the waist, and, if she made any more words, swore that he would fling her out of the window.

† I know well that you are a real she devil but I'll have you know that I am Beelzebub the lord of Devils.

Mainwaring concludes his account with the amusing observation; 'It is to be noted, that this was formerly one of the methods of executing criminals in some parts of Germany'. Despite this early *contretemps*, Cuzzoni continued as Handel's *prima donna* (singing the role of Cleopatra in *Giulio Cesare* and the lead in *Rodelinda*) until the arrival of another celebrated soprano, Faustina Bordoni in May 1726 (fig.56). Although the Royal Academy had now engaged three of the greatest singers in Europe (Senesino, Cuzzoni and Faustina), it was to prove disastrous, when the inevitable rivalry between the two sopranos developed into open warfare. In a hopeless attempt to dispel their hostility, Handel wrote the score of *Alessandro* (first performed 5 May 1726) providing equal opportunities for his two female leads to display their individual talents (fig.57). Later, during the run of Handel's *Admeto* (first performed 31 January 1727) this hostility, encouraged and exacerbated by audience partisanship, caused uproar in the theatre and resulted in the immediate publication of satirical pamphlets (fig.58). The two sopranos finally came to blows on stage on 6 June 1727, during Bononcini's *Astianatte*.

Handel's attitude towards his soloists and orchestra appears to have been very dictatorial. Burney recalled that at 'the close of an air, the

fig.55
John Vanderbank, *Caricature of Senesino, Cuzzoni and Berenstadt* (possibly Handel's *Flavio* or Ariosti's *Coriolano*), etching, c.1723, 183 × 260mm.

The Byrne Collection,
Handel House Collections Trust.

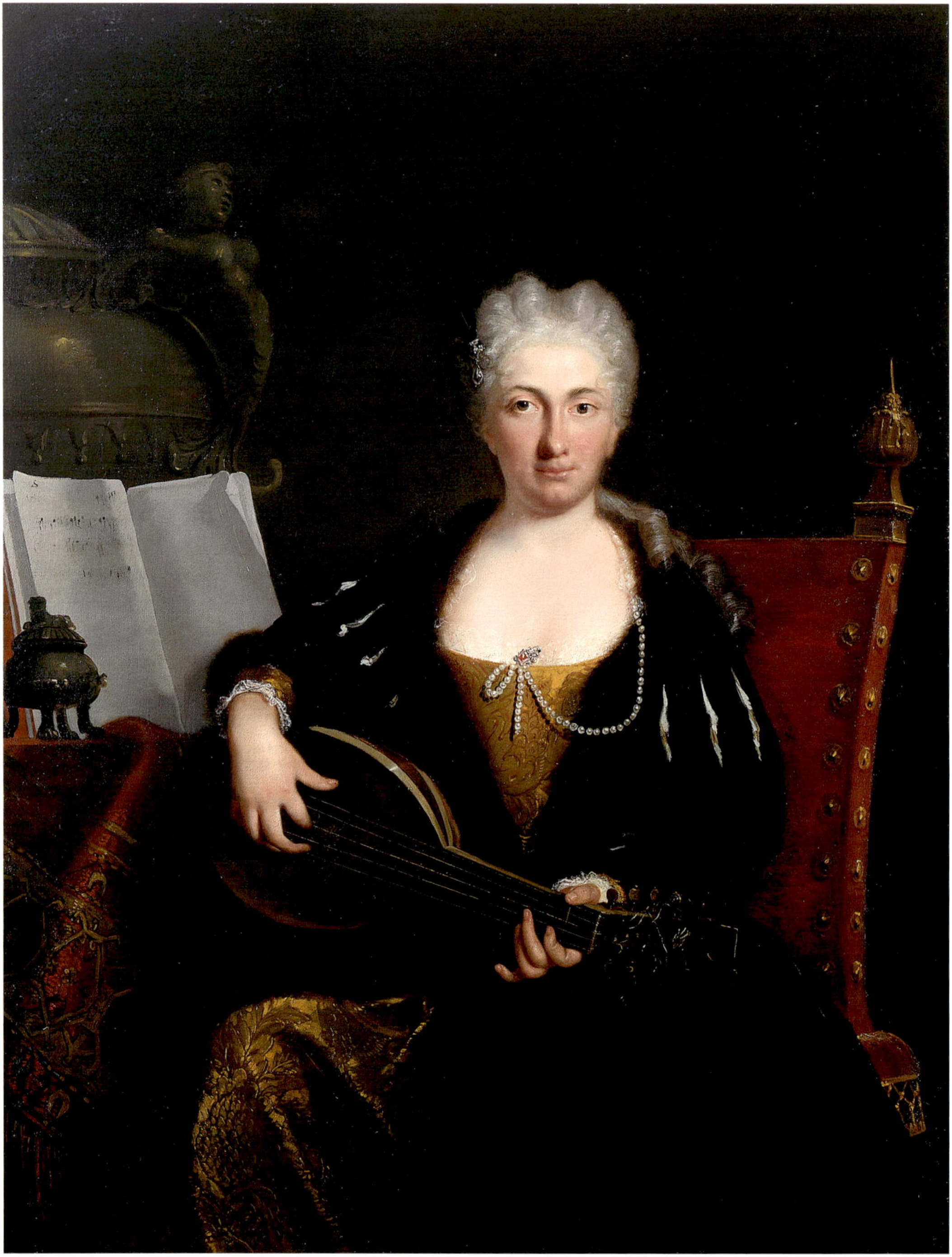

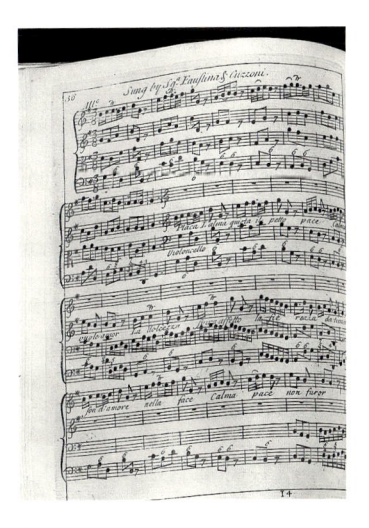

fig.56 [opposite]
Bartolomeo Nazari, *Faustina Bordoni*, oil on canvas, c.1734, 134 × 106mm.

Handel House Collections Trust.

fig.57 [above]
Placa l'alma…sung by Sga Faustina and Cuzzoni from *Alexander* [Alessandro]. *An Opera…*, printed score, 1st ed., pub. John Cluer, 1726, London.

The Byrne Collection,
Handel House Collections Trust.

fig.58
Title page to An Epistle from S[ignor]e S[enesin]o to S[ignor]a F[austin]a, anonymous, printed pamphlet, pub. James Roberts, 1727, London.

Handel House Collections Trust.

fig.59
John Faber after George Knapton, *Giovanni Carestini*, mezzotint engraving, 1735, 290 × 254mm.

The Byrne Collection,
Handel House Collections Trust.

voice with which he used to cry out, CHORUS! Was extremely formidable indeed'. As the threatened defenestration of Cuzzoni suggests, his imperious behaviour was particularly directed against his Italian soloists who could be forgiven for considering themselves more important than Handel himself due to the extraordinarily high fees they commanded in London. Bearing in mind the operatic egos he was dealing with (Faustina and Cuzzoni being only two) it is little wonder that Handel attempted to maintain absolute command. Mainwaring infers that his manner caused the departure from Handel's opera company of Senesino, the most celebrated castrato in London prior to the arrival of Farinelli in 1734; 'The perfect authority which HANDEL maintained over the singers and the band, or rather the total subjection in which he held them, was of more consequence than can well be imagined.' Senesino arrived in London in September 1720 and until the early 1730s, sang the lead in the first performances of Handel's Royal Academy operas including *Ottone*, *Flavio*, *Giulio Cesare* and *Tamerlano*. The singer's popularity, particularly amongst the female members of the opera-going public, prompted John Gay to write, with more than a hint of irony, that Senesino was 'daily voted to be the greatest man that ever lived.' In contrast to this universal adulation, Handel is recorded as having called him 'a damned fool' during one heated exchange. Their relationship appears to have settled into an uneasy truce until Senesino's defection to the Opera of the Nobility in 1733. To replace him, Handel brought in another castrato, Giovanni Carestini (c.1705–60) (fig.59) who sang the male lead in both *Ariodante* and *Alcina*. Carestini, like Cuzzoni, experienced the full might of Handel's rage when he refused to sing the aria *Verdi prati* from *Alcina*.

Handel had a less turbulent relationship with his English singers. One of his earliest encounters was with the great bass singer and composer Richard Leveridge (1670/1–1758) who had been a member of the theatre company for which Henry Purcell (1659–95) had written music in the 1690s. For Handel, he sang in the first performances of *Il pastor fido* and *Teseo* at what was then the Queen's Theatre. Like

Leveridge, Anastasia Robinson (c.1692–1755) (fig.60) was one of the few English singers to perform for the Royal Academy. Between 1714 and her retirement in 1724 she sang soprano and contralto roles in *Radamisto*, *Florldante*, *Ottone*, *Flavio* and *Giulio Cesare*. It seems that, unlike her Italian colleagues, she wisely favoured a non-confrontational approach; explaining her concerns to influential friends and imploring them to speak to Handel on her behalf. Robinson considered herself miscast in *Ottone* and had made suggestions to a friend as to how her part might be changed to suit her more placid temperament. In a second letter she writes;

You have hear'd my new Part, and the more I look at it, the more I find it is impossible for me to sing it; I dare not ask Mr Hendell to change the Songs for fear he should suspect (as he is very likely) every other reason but the true one. Do you believe if I was to wait on Lady Darlinton to beg her to use that power over him (which to be sure she must have) to get it done, that she would give her self that trouble, would she have compassion on a distressed Damsell that they are endeavouring to make an abominable Scold of (in spite of her Vertuous inclinations to the contrary) as to hinder the wrong they would do her [?]

Her letter offers further proof of Handel's authoritarian approach towards his singers and particularly his music.

Amongst his English singers, Handel's favourite appears to have been Susanna Cibber (1714–66) (fig.61) sister of the composer Thomas Arne. Burney recalled that Handel 'was very fond of Mrs. Cibber, whose voice and manners had softened his severity for her want of musical knowledge.' On 13 April 1742 she sang in the first performance of *Messiah* in Dublin during which her emotional interpretation of *He was despised* prompted the Rev Patrick Delany (later, husband of Mrs Pendarves) to cry out, 'Woman, for this, be all they sins forgiven!' Another of Handel's singers who, like Cibber, was more famed as an actress, was Kitty Clive (fig.62) for whom Handel wrote the song *I like the am'rous youth that's free* which she performed during the play

fig.60
John Faber after John Vanderbank, *Anastasia Robinson*, mezzotint engraving, 1727, 315 × 250mm
Private Collection.

fig.61 [above]
John Faber after Thomas Hudson, *Susanna Cibber*, mezzotint engraving, 1746, 270 × 225mm.

The Byrne Collection,
House Collections Trust.

fig.62 [above right]
Alexander van Aken after [Jeremiah Davison and] **Joseph van Aken**, *Kitty Clive*, mezzotint engraving, 1735, 320 × 250mm.

The Byrne Collection,
Handel House Collections Trust.

"Universal Passion" at Drury Lane in 1737. For a short period she sang in Handel's oratorios singing in the first performance of *L'Allegro*, in the first London performance of *Messiah* and taking the role of Dalila in *Samson* in 1743.

From the 1730s onwards there are references to Handel rehearsing operas and oratorios at his Brook Street house. Donald Burrows has suggested that for those works first performed at the Covent Garden Theatre in the 1730s and 1740s (such as *Alcina* and *Solomon*), rehearsing at his own house (or indeed at other venues such as Carlton House) may have become necessary because Handel shared the theatre with an actors company, and therefore would not have had unlimited access to rehearsal space on site. Our knowledge of these rehearsals comes from the letters and diaries of Handel's intimate friends who were present. In a letter dated 27 April 1734, Mrs Pendarves writes 'Yesterday morning at the rehearsal of a most delightful opera at Mr Handel's called Sosarme, which is acted tonight'. Again on 12 April 1735 she writes, 'Yesterday morning my sister [Ann Granville] and I went with Mrs. Donellan to Mr Handel's house to hear the first rehearsal of the new opera Alcina', revealing the extraordinary privilege and access such friends were accorded by the composer. In her account of the latter rehearsal, Mrs Pendarves refers to Strada (*fl.*1719–40), Handel's leading soprano from 1729 until 1737, who took the lead part in the opera.

Handel accompanied on the harpsichord, in Mrs Pendarves words, 'Whilst Mr. Handel was playing his part, I could not help thinking him a necromancer in the midst of his own enchantments.'

Other references to rehearsals at Brook Street can be found in the correspondence and journal of George Harris, the younger brother of James and Thomas, all of whom were friends and supporters of Handel. In a letter to Elizabeth Harris (dated 8 February 1746) he writes, 'Yesterday morning I was at Handel's house to hear the rehearsal of his new Occasional Oratorio.' The rehearsal probably involved Handel's soloists, the French soprano La Francesina (Elizabetta Du Parc) (d.1773), the bass Henry Theodore Reinhold (d.1751), the tenor John Beard (c.1717–91), the principal instrumentalists including the Dutch violinist and composer Willem de Fesch, who was 'first fiddle' (fig.63), and chorus leaders. Francesina (fig.64) had sung in *Serse* and in Handel's two last operas *Imeneo* and *Deidamia* (1740/1). In 1744 she took the lead in *Semele* but her association with Handel ended in the same year that this rehearsal took place. John Beard (fig.65) sang as a choir boy in the 1732 production of *Esther*, leaving the Chapel Royal in 1734 to join Handel's opera company. An observer wrote that 'Mr Handell is so full of his [Beard's] Praises that he says he will surprise the Town with his performances before the Winter is over.' In a professional relationship which lasted until Handel's death, Beard performed in both operas (creating parts in *Ariodante*, *Alcina* and *Giustino*) and oratorios, including the first London performance of *Messiah* (and subsequent Foundling Hospital performances in the 1750s) and creating the title roles in *Samson* (1743), *Belshazzar* (1745), *Judas Maccabaeus* (1746) and *Jephtha* (1752). George Harris seems to have been a not infrequent observer of rehearsals at Brook Street during the 1740s, as he also notes in his diary on Saturday, 4 March 1749, 'Solomon, rehearsal, Handel's, Brook Street' and later on Tuesday 21 March, 'Heard Messiah rehearsed, Handel's'.

As the front room on the first floor was the largest room in Handel's house, it is certain that all the Brook Street rehearsals mentioned above

fig.63
Andrea Soldi, *Willem de Fesch*, oil on canvas, c.1750, 765 × 635mm.

The Byrne Collection,
Handel House Collections Trust.

fig.64
John Faber after George Knapton,
La Francesina (Elizabetta Du Parc), mezzotint engraving, 1737, 289 × 222mm.

National Portrait Gallery, London.

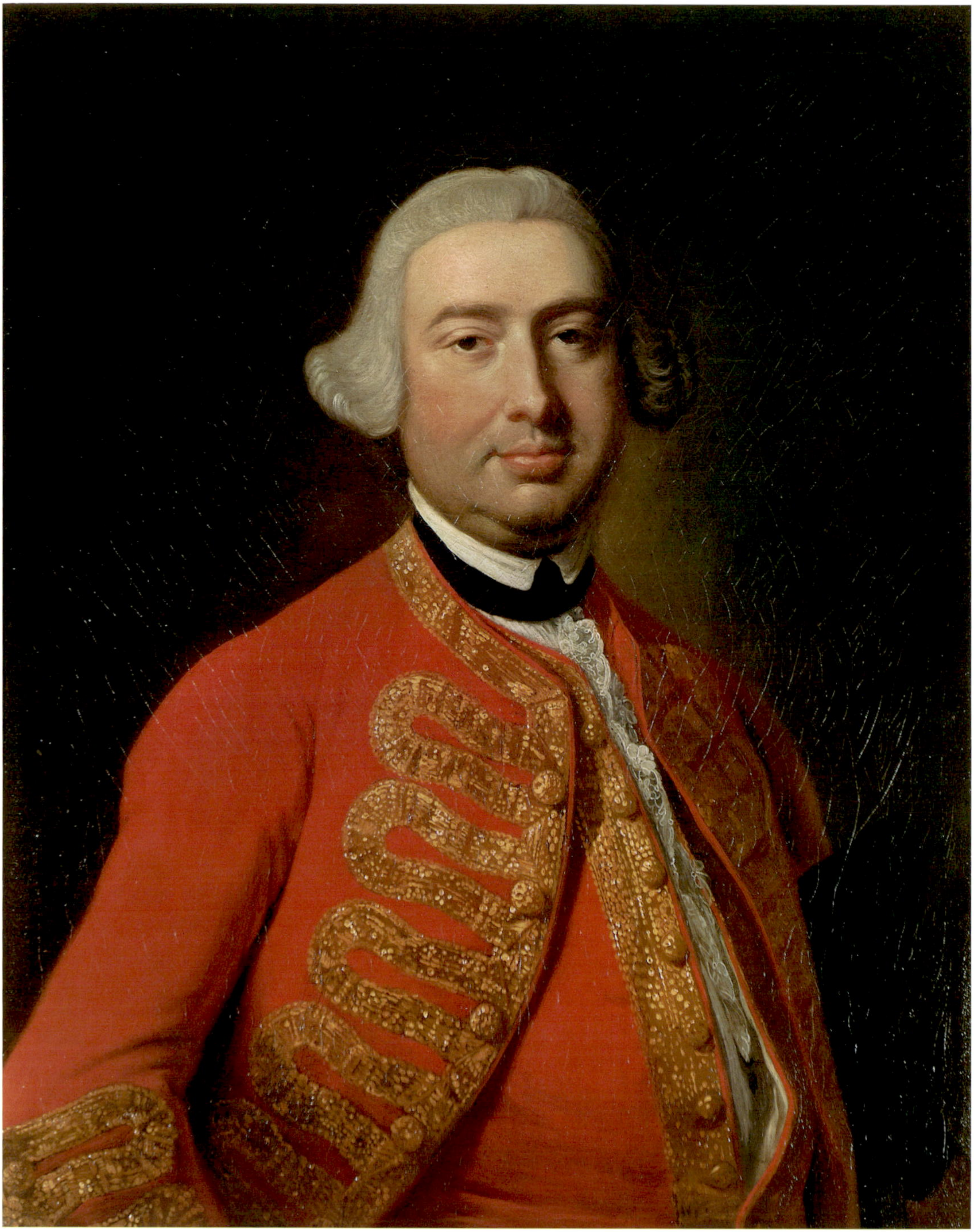

occurred here. However, even the largest room at Brook Street was modest, bearing in mind the amount of people who may have been present for rehearsals. Burney recounts a conversation with the violinist Abraham Brown (leader of the King's Band and listed as the lead violinist at performances of *Messiah* at the Foundling Hospital in the late 1750s) during which Brown recalled, 'how civilly he had been attended by him [ie Handel] to the door, and how carefully cautioned, after being heated by a crowded room and hard labour, at the rehearsals in Brook-street, not to stir without a chair.' 'Chair' in this context probably refers to a popular mode of transport (ie a sedan chair) rather than a seat.

However, it is tempting to suggest that the large amount of seat furniture which is listed in the 1759 inventory (over forty chairs – predominantly rush-matted – half of which were on the first and second floors) existed in the event of a rehearsal, where large numbers of musicians and/or guests required seating at one time. Further, although the inventory is not complete, the front room on the first floor contained a surprisingly small amount of furniture – '2 Wall[e] Round card tables 7 Wall[e] Matted Chairs & a Leather Stool' – again suggesting that either one or both of Handel's larger instruments had been located in this room. Handel clearly continued to use his house as a rehearsal space right up to the year before his death, as the following entry in the diary of John Baker, a barrister (dated 2 Mar 1758) reveals; 'Mr Banister and I in his chariot to Handel's, Lower Brook Street, where heard rehearsed the Oratorio of 'Judas Maccabaeus', by Frasi, Miss Young als [alias] Miss Scott, Cassandra Frederica, Beard, Champness, Baildon etc.' In fact, this select rehearsal occurred the day before the performance.

Brook Street was probably a busy thoroughfare even in Handel's day and the stable yard at the rear of Handel's house must have added to the general noise and bustle of the immediate area. But even so, considering Handel's house formed part of a terrace, its use as a rehearsal space – let alone the regular playing of a "little" house organ – suggests that at times Handel must have been a very noisy neighbour.

fig.65 [opposite]
Thomas Hudson, *John Beard*, oil on canvas, c.1743, 742 × 622mm.

Gerald Coke Handel Collection.
Photograph, National Portrait Gallery, London.

6 Composition

Anthony Hicks

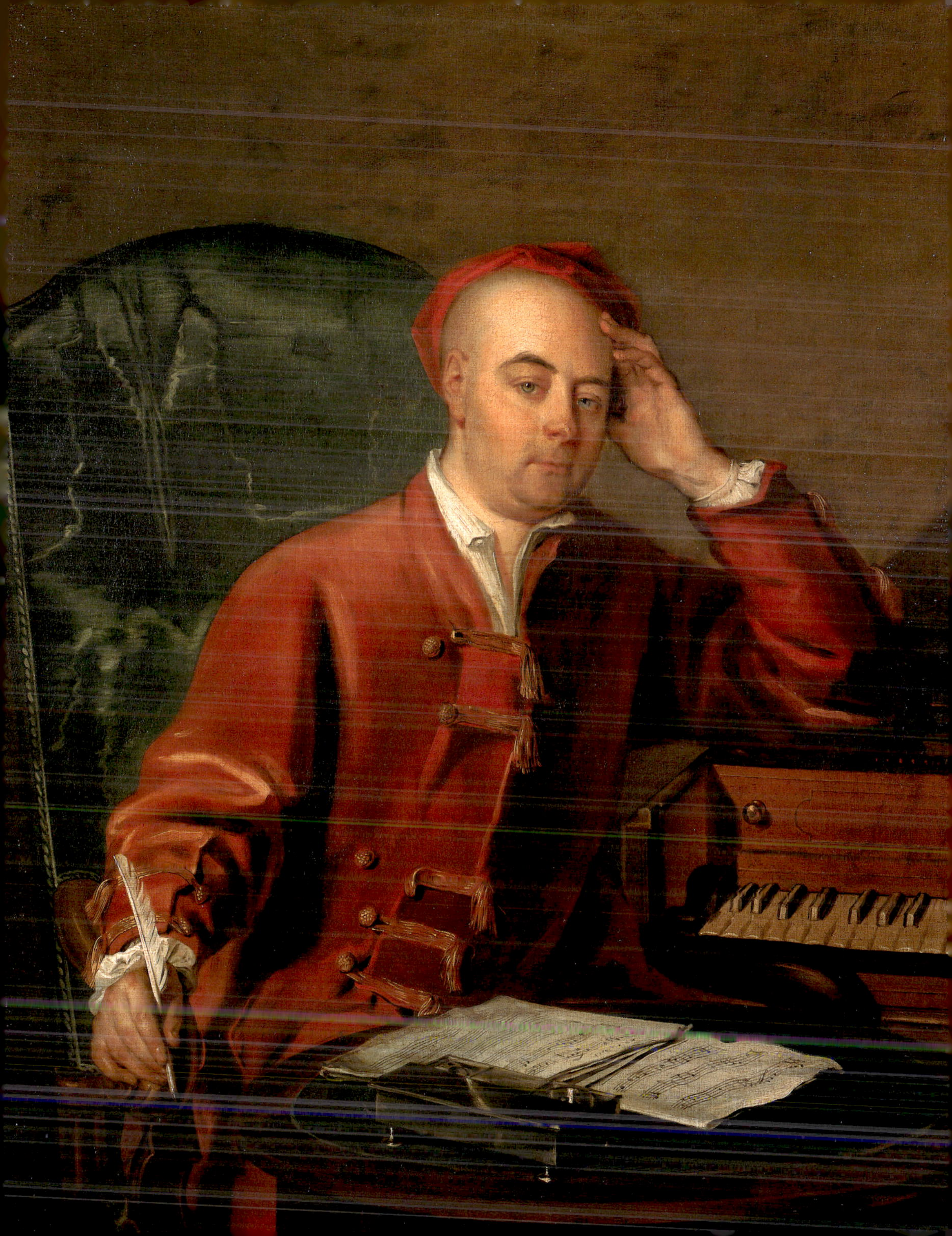

fig.66 [previous page]
Philip Mercier, *Handel*, oil on canvas, c. 1730, 1270 × 1016mm.

The Viscount FitzHarris 1969 Setlement. Photograph, National Portrait Gallery, London.

COMPOSITION

THE ACCOUNT OF Handel's early years in Mainwaring's *Memoirs* – almost certainly based on the composer's own reminiscences – mentions the boy's ability as a keyboard player as the first sign of his musical gifts, developed despite his father's opposition. We may guess that he soon began to improvise at the keyboard, a facility for which he was greatly admired in later life. His first efforts at composition on paper were probably made when he became a pupil of Zachow, the organist at the Marienkirche at Halle. Mainwaring says that he was then seven years old, and that 'by the time he was nine he began to compose the church service [ie a church cantata] for voices and instruments, and from that time actually did compose a service every week for three years successively'. More probably Handel became Zachow's scholar when he was nine (as implied in the short biography in J G Walther's *Musicalisches Lexicon* of 1732) and began to compose church cantatas a year or two after that.

Sadly, none of these early cantatas have survived, but we can be sure that when Handel left Halle in 1703 to join the orchestra of the opera house in Hamburg, he was already conscious of his worth as a composer and was seeking new outlets for his talent. The temporary absence of Reinhard Keiser, the leading Hamburg composer, gave Handel the chance to compose his first opera, *Almira*, on a text originally intended for Keiser. Its sprawling mix of several elements, with courtly dances and comic episodes supplementing the many arias (some in Italian, some in German) was determined by the current fashion in Hamburg, and Handel's distinct voice emerges only intermittently; but the signs of a dramatic composer, able to portray in music the emotions of his characters, are clearly present. Thus when Handel went to Italy sometime in 1705/6 he was an experienced composer of choral church music and had a good understanding of the opera of the period, dominated by solo arias which had to satisfy the whims of singers and the tastes of audiences as well as the composer's own artistic conscience.

Handel continued these two streams of compositional activity separately through his years in Italy (1705/6–10), but with emphasis on works for solo voice. His only choral music of this period consists of settings of three Latin psalms for Vespers (including the splendid *Dixit Dominus*) and the final movement of an Italian sacred cantata. The public performance of opera was forbidden in Rome, where he was mainly based, but a highly operatic style of Italian oratorio was cultivated instead. His two operas written in Italy were therefore composed for Florence (*Rodrigo*) and Venice (*Agrippina*), but for Rome he produced two brilliant oratorios *Il trionfo del Tempo e del Disinganno* and *La Resurrezione*. It was however another musical form, one new to him, which occupied Handel most consistently throughout this period: the Italian secular cantata. Some of his cantatas are large-scale pieces with orchestra, but most are short works for a single voice and an instrumental bass, with just two or three arias, a valuable form for experimentation. Such pieces were often presented at weekly *soirées* in the palaces of patrons, sometimes in response to an artistic challenge, so that the words might be written, the music composed and the completed cantatas sung all in the course of a single evening. The little cantata composed by Handel to words by Cardinal Pamphili, praising the composer as 'greater than Orpheus', may well have been produced in such circumstances, since the poet says that he cannot produce 'in an instant' verses worthy of Handel's music.

Italian opera and music for the church continued to be Handel's two areas of major activity during his first twenty years in England, the church music of course being English and mainly associated with ceremonial occasions such as the celebration of the Peace of Utrecht in 1713 or the coronation of King George II and Queen Caroline in 1727. Eventually, in the series of English oratorios and musical dramas begun with the London production of *Esther* in 1732, Handel found a concept in which the two strands could be united within the dramatic framework he always favoured.

Both for opera and oratorio Handel usually worked with great speed during the initial stage of composition, producing a draft score of a whole act of an opera or oratorio in a matter of days; this was common

fig.67

Memoirs of the Life of the Late George Frederic Handel… by John Mainwaring, printed book with marginalia by Charles Jennens, pub. Robert and James Dodsley, 1760, London, p.63.

The Byrne Collection,
Handel House Collections Trust.

In this section of Mainwaring's biography, which covers Handel's career in Italy, Jennens notes in the margin, 'Handel told me that the words of Il Trionfo &c. were written by Cardinal Pamphili, & added, "an old Fool!" I ask'd Why Fool? because he wrote an Oratorio? perhaps you will call me fool for the same reason!" He answer'd "So I would, if you flatter'd me as He did."

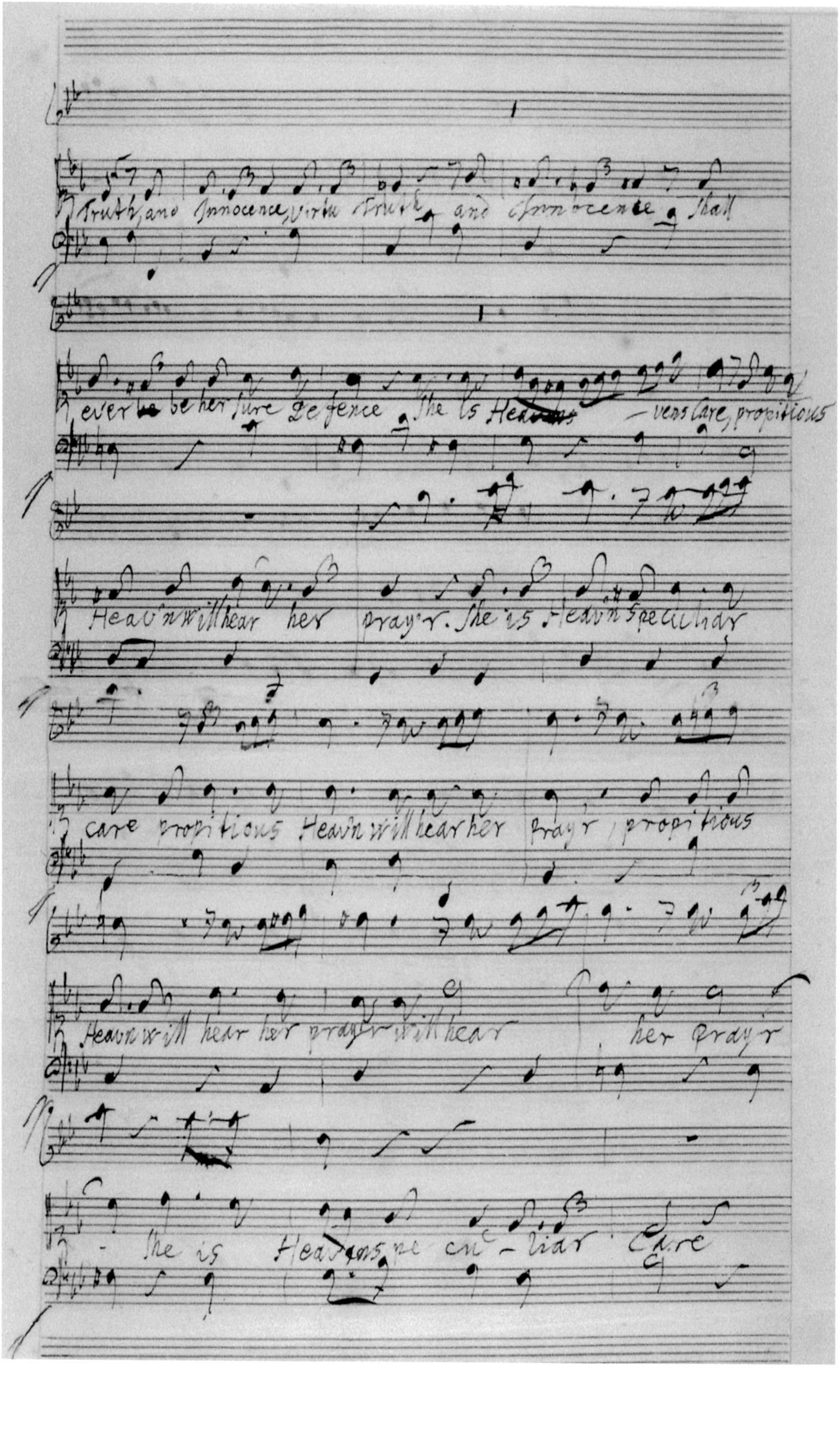

practice for composers of his time. Details of orchestration and the setting of the recitatives followed shortly afterwards. Much less typical was Handel's habit of making substantial revisions before the work reached performance, possibly including the re-ordering of scenes and other structural changes as well as the more usual adjustment or replacement of arias to accommodate the needs of the singers. The opera *Tamerlano*, for example, was subjected to major revision after Handel had obtained a new version of the libretto with a fine death scene for the tragic character of Bajazet; and in *Alcina* Handel added the newly-invented role of Oberto for the talented boy treble William Savage after the first version of the score had been completed. Considerations of overall balance and theatrical effect were of great importance to Handel, and explain his occasional annoyance with singers – the famous examples are the soprano Cuzzoni and the castrato Carestini– who objected to singing dramatically appropriate arias he had provided for them (see chapter 5)

The librettos for the London operas were generally adapted from those of earlier productions in Italy, allowing Handel and his literary collaborators a reasonably free hand in reshaping them to suit his artistic judgement and the expectations of English audiences not fluent in Italian. In the case of the English oratorios and other choral works in similar style – a form which Handel largely invented, with little precedent to guide him – the librettos were usually newly written and were provided by a circle of friends eager to engage the composer's interest and to bring out the full range of his genius. Charles Jennens (fig.69) was among the most important of these. His first libretto was that for *Saul* (1738–39), the most powerful of the early dramatic oratorios. A year later he worked directly with Handel himself in adapting and extending a draft for what became *L'Allegro, il Penseroso ed il Moderato* (1740), a selection of Milton's verses prepared by another influential friend, James Harris of Salisbury. Its evocation of contrasted moods through idealised visions of the English landscape inspired some of Handel's most exquisite music. Around the same time

fig.68 [opposite]
Page of an inserted aria 'Virtue, truth and innocence' for a performance of *Esther* in 1751, in Handel's autograph.

The Byrne Collection,
Handel House Collections Trust.

fig.69
Thomas Hudson, *Charles Jennens*,
oil on canvas, c.1744, 1230 × 1015mm.
Handel House Collections Trust.

fig.70 [opposite]
Autograph letter concerning *Belshazzar* and *Messiah* from Handel to Charles Jennens at Gopsall, 19 July 1744.
The Byrne Collection,
Handel House Collections Trust.

fig.71 [below]
Envelope (with seal) addressed to Charles Jennens (junior) Esq at Gopsall, near Atherstone Leicestershire by Handel.
The Byrne Collection,
Handel House Collections Trust.

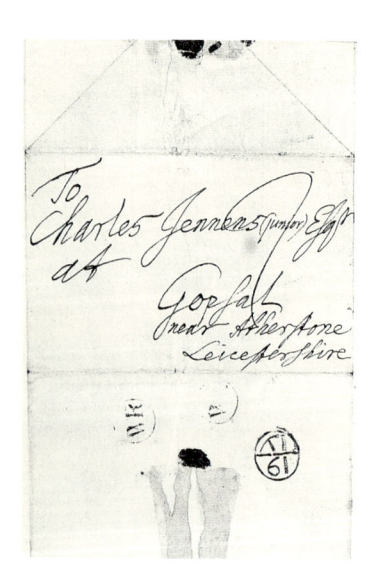

Jennens also had the idea of a 'sacred oratorio' designed for performance in Passion Week, based on texts compiled from the Bible. This was, of course, *Messiah*, set by Handel in 1741 (though not achieving its final form until 1750). Here the sublimity of the theme and the lofty language of the English Bible found their match in the music, still the most popular of all oratorios. Jennens's final libretto, for *Belshazzar* (1744–45), gave Handel the opportunity to create a vivid historical epic. *Messiah* is exceptional in that its verbal text hardly changed through several musical revisions, whereas Jennens had to respond (sometimes grudgingly) to the composer's demands for textual changes in *Saul* and *Belshazzar*. Subsequently Handel also had good service from Dr Thomas Morell (fig 72) as a provider of librettos, with *Theodora* (1749–50), the moving story of two doomed Christian martyrs, arguably the finest product of their collaboration.

Handel not only found inspiration in texts but in music itself. Like most composers, he frequently reused or reworked elements of his own

July 25. 1744

Dear Sir

At my arrival in London, which was Yesterday, J immediately perused the Act of the Oratorio with which You favour'd me, and, the little time only J had it, gives me great Pleasure. Your reasons for the Lenght of the first act are intirely satisfactory to me, and it is likewise my Opinion to have the following Acts short. J shall be very glad and much obliged to You, if you will soon favour me with the remaining Acts. Be pleased to point out these passages in the Oratorio which You think require altering.

J desire my humble Respects and thanks to My Lord Guernsey for his many Civility's to me — and believe me to be with the greatest Respect

Your
most obedient and most humble Servant
George Frideric Handel

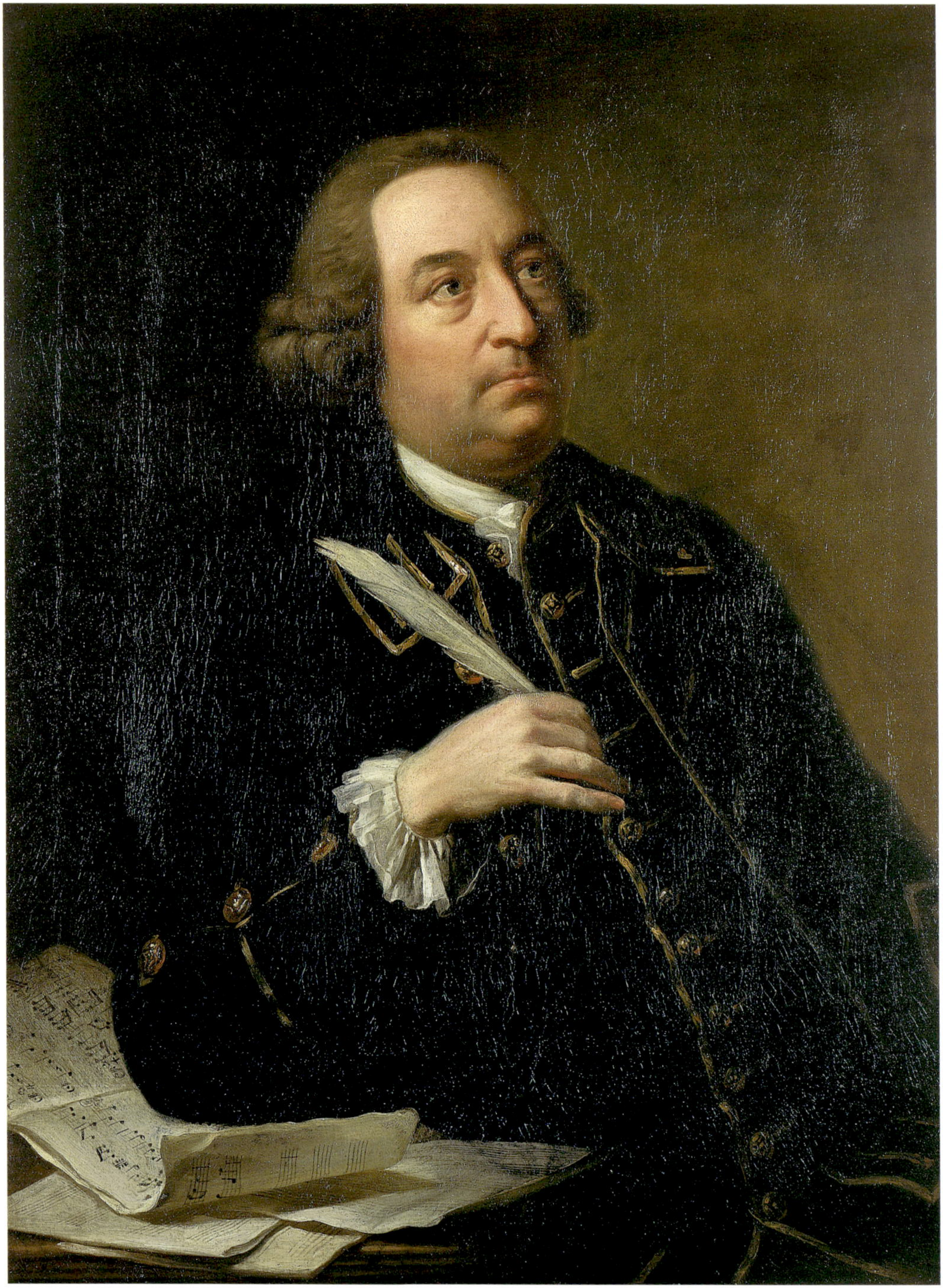

compositions in later works – sometimes just a phrase or a theme, sometimes a whole movement – especially when the originals would be unfamiliar to the new audience. Unique among the great composers, however, was his habit of 'borrowing', or using musical material from other composers' works. This is detectable in his earliest music for Italy (which draws upon Keiser's Hamburg operas) and is present in most of his compositions right up to *Jephtha* (1751–52), in which the Act 1 duet is astonishingly based on a duet in a serenata by Baldassare Galuppi (1706–85), written only the previous year. The borrowings do not diminish Handel's stature: instead, the ways in which he reworks or finds new contexts for the borrowed material often confirm his genius and give insight into how music makes its effect. (Unfortunately, discussion of the subject has been confined largely to scholarly publication, but with the aid of aural examples it can and should be opened to a wider public.)

From his time in Italy to the end of his life Handel was fairly diligent in keeping the autograph manuscripts of his music. They finally amounted to over 100 volumes – about two-thirds written at Brook Street – and provide an intimate record of his working life as a composer. The majority are now in the former Royal Collection in the British Library, having passed to Handel's chief copyist J C Smith the elder and then to his son, (fig.73), who gave them to King George III. (It was the younger Smith who helped Handel add 'new' music to his oratorios after he went blind in 1754, apparently composing the music himself under Handel's supervision and using existing Handel themes.) The autographs graphically demonstrate Handel's working methods, showing the extent of his revisions and confirming – despite their untidy appearance – his care for detail. They do not always represent

fig.72
James Basire after William Hogarth, *Thomas Morell*, engraving, pub. 1762, 197 × 149mm.

The Byrne Collection,
Handel House Collections Trust.

fig.73 [opposite]
Johann Zoffany, *John Christopher Smith the younger*, oil on canvas, c.1763, 889 × 679mm.

Gerald Coke Handel Collection.
Photograph, National Portrait Gallery, London.

fig.74
The opening of the Hallelujah Chorus from Handel's autograph score.
British Library (R.M.20 f.2).

Handel's final thoughts, however. In the case of operas and oratorios his practice was to have an early copy made by a senior copyist (J C Smith the elder from about 1720 onwards), and it was in that working copy, or 'conducting score', that further amendments were generally made, both before first performance and for later revivials. Happily many of the conducting scores also survive, the bulk of them having been saved from the scrap heap in the 1850s by a Bristol book dealer, Thomas Kerslake. They were acquired by the Hamburg State Library in 1868 at the instigation of Friedrich Chrysander, the nineteenth-century editor of Handel's collected works, and remain there today. The actual performing material used by Handel's singers and orchestral players is unfortunately almost all lost, though there are a few interesting exceptions (such as the first desk cello part for *Alexander's Feast*, in the library of the Royal College of Music).

It is in the autographs that we come closest to seeing Handel in the actual act of composition, working quickly, yet frequently refining his initial thoughts with anything from a tiny improvement of a phase to the replacement of a substantial passage of music. A brief glance at the autograph of one of the most famous passages in all Handel – the opening of the Hallelujah Chorus in *Messiah* (fig.74) – is itself revealing. At the start the uppermost and lowest instrumental lines (for the first violins – 'V 1.' – and the bass instruments) appear slightly thicker than the rest, showing that they were written first. Handel then went back to 'fill in' the score with the other instrumental lines. At the same time he lowered the first note of the first violins an octave and added the little 'run up' to the entry of the chorus, each alteration giving forward impetus to the music line. Handel never attempted to create explicit monuments to his art in the manner of his great contemporary J S Bach – there are no Handelian equivalents of the 'Goldberg Variations' or 'The Art of Fugue' – but his compositions consistently bear witness to a humane musical mastery in which formal coherence and emotional power are inextricably combined.

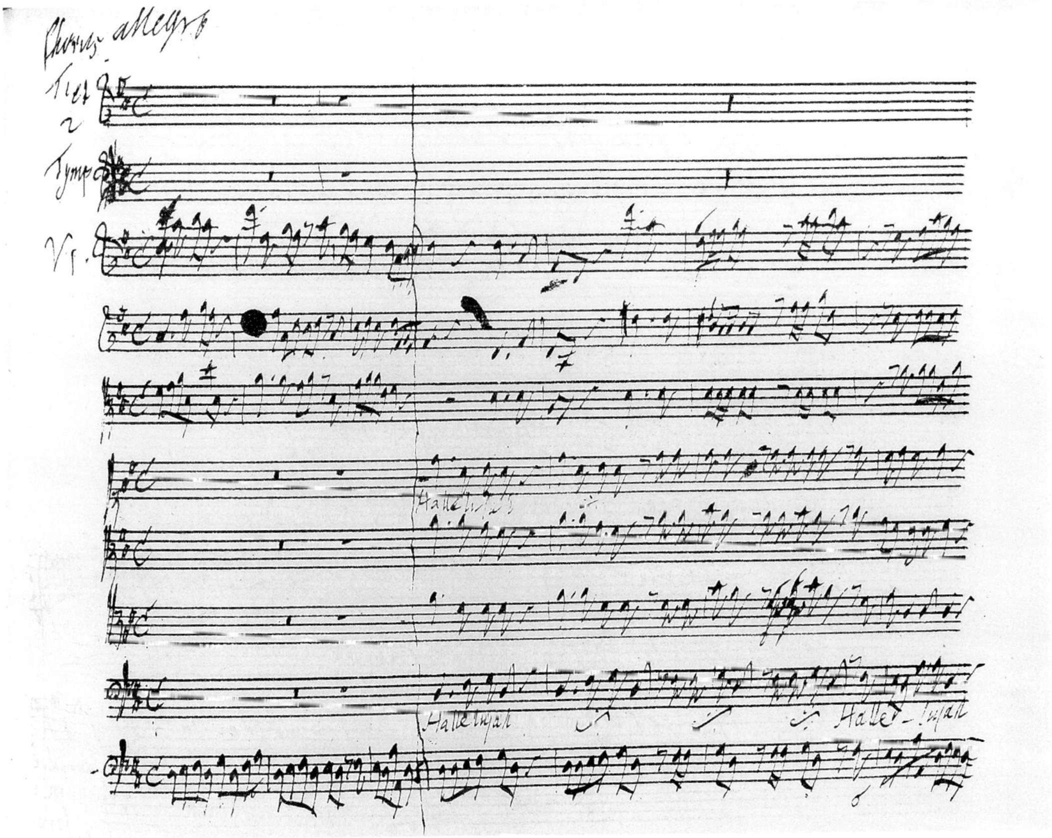
Chorus. allegro
Tymp
Hallelujah
Halle-lujah

Index

illustration page numbers in bold

A
Academy of Vocal [Ancient] Music 39
Aix-la-Chapelle 14
Anne, Queen of Great Britain 10, 11, 39, 41
Ariosti, Attilio 39
Arne, [Dr] Thomas Augustine 44–46, **44**, 69
Arnold, [Dr] Samuel 58

B
Bach, Johann Sebastian 56, 84
Baker, John 73
Barnes, George 23, 29, 30
Bath 14
Beard, John 71, **73**
Beggar's Opera, The **37**, *38*, 43, 44
Bononcini, Giovanni 15, 38, 65
Bordoni, Faustina 35, 43, 65, **66**, **67**, 68
Britton, Thomas 40, **41**,
Brook Street, No. 25:
  composition 24, 83
  death of Handel at 58
  entertaining at 52
  inventory of 26, *26*, 32–3, *32*, 56, 73
  rehearsals at 24, 70–73
  restoration 26–35
Brown, Abraham 54
Brydges, James (Earl of Carnarvon/Duke of Chandos) 15, 42
Burlington, (Richard Boyle) Earl of 15, 16, 38, 42
Burlington House 15, 42
Burney, [Dr] Charles 50, **50**, 51, 54, 56, 61, 65

C
Cannons Park 15, 42
Carestini, Giovanni 68, *68*, 79
Caroline, Queen 13, 77
Chapel Royal 13, 23, 71
Chandos, Duke of (see Brydges, James)
Chrysander, Friedrich 84
Cibber [Arne], Susanna 69, **70**
Clive, Catherine [Kitty] 69, **70**
Corelli, Archangelo 10

Covent Garden Theatre 16, 17, **17**, 18
Coxe, William 50, 51
Culloden, Battle, of 18
Cumberland, (William) Duke of 18
Cuzzoni, Francesca 43, 64–5, **65**, 68, 79

D
De Fesch, Willem 71, **71**
Dublin 14, 18, 56, 69
Dubourg, Matthew 56
Du Burk, John 26, 30

E
Enraged Musician, The (William Hogarth) **44**

F
Farinelli [Carlo Broschi] 16
Faustina (see Bordoni, Faustina)
Flörcke, Johanne Frederike 52
Florence 10, 76–77
Foundling Hospital 19, 47, 54, **55**, 71, 73
Francesina [Elizabetta Du Parc] 71, **71**
Francis Matthew Schutz in his bed (William Hogarth) **33**
Frederick, Prince of Wales 16
'Fund for the Support of Decay'd Musicians' 54

G
Galliard, John Ernest 39, 40
Galuppi, Baldassare 83
Gay, John 43, 68
Geminiani, Francesco 39
George I, (Georg Ludwig) King of Great Britain, Elector of Hanover 10, 11, **13**, 41
George II, King of Great Britain 13, 77
George III, King of Great Britain 61, 83
Goupy, Joseph 52
Granville, Bernard 24, 55, 58
Green Park (see Handel, Fireworks Music)

H
Halle 10, 52, 76
Hamburg 50, 76
Hamilton, Newburgh 46
Handel, George Frideric, works
  Aci, Galatea e Polifemo, 10
  Acis and Galatea 15, 43
  Admeto 65
  Agrippina 10, 77

  Alcina 16, 68, 70, 71, 79
  Alessandro 65, **67**
  Alexander Balus,
  Alexander's Feast 17, 24, **25**, 84
  L'Allegro, il Penseroso ed il Moderato 18, 70, 79
  Almira 10, 76
  Amadigi 14
  Ariodante 16, 68, 71
  As pants the Hart 13
  Athalia 17
  Belshazzar 35, 71, 80
  'Chandos' [Cannons] Anthems 13, 15
  'Chandos' [Cannons] Te Deum 15
  Coronation Anthems 13, 77
  Deidamia 71
  Dixit Dominus 77
  Esther 17, 35, 42, 71, 77, **78**
  Fireworks Music 14, 19, **46**, 47
  Flavio 68, 69
  Floridante 69
  Foundling Hospital Anthem 54
  Giulio Cesare 15, **16**, 65, 68, 69
  Giustino, 71
  'Harmonious Blacksmith, The' 15
  'I like the am'rous youth that's free' 69
  Imeneo 71
  Israel in Egypt 17
  Jephtha 19, 55, 56, 71, 80
  Judas Maccabaeus 18, 46, 55, 71
  Messiah 18, 19, 35, 69, 70, 71, 73, 80, 84, **85**
  Occasional Oratorio 71
  Ottone 64, 68, 69
  Pastor fido, Il 14, 68
  Radamisto 69
  'Rejoice, the Lord is King' 13
  Resurrezione, La 10
  Rinaldo 11, **12**, 40
  Rodelinda 65
  Rodrigo 10
  Samson 18, 56, 70, 71
  Saul 17, 79, 80
  Semele, (The Story of) 71
  Serse 17, 71
  Solomon 70, 71
  Song (Ode) for St Cecilia's Day, *Sosarme* 70
  Tamerlano 15, 68, 77
  Teseo 14, 68
  Theodora 55, 80
  Trionfo del Tempo e del Disinganno, Il 10, 77
  'Utrecht' Te Deum and Jubilate 13, 77
  Water Music 13
  Zadok the Priest 13
Handel, G F, images of:
  Faber, John after Thomas Hudson, mezzotint engraving **52**
  after Goupy, Joseph, The Charming Brute, engraving 52, **53**

Heath, James after Biagio Rebecca, Apotheosis of Handel, **60**
Houbraken, Jacobus, engraving **25**
after Hudson, Thomas, oil on canvas **49**
Kyte, Francis, oil on canvas **9**
Mercier, Philip, oil on canvas 24–5, **75**
Roubiliac, L-F, Cast of Death (?) Mask, plaster **59**
Roubiliac, L-F, Monument in Westminster Abbey 19, **19**, 47, 51
Roubiliac, L-F, Vauxhall Gardens Statue, 47, **52**
Handel Commemoration (1784) 58, **61**
Handel's House (John Buckler) **21**
Händel, Dorothea Elizabeth 52
Händel, Georg Friedrich 54, 76
Hanover 10, 11, 50, 54
Harris, George 55, 71
Harris, James (of Salisbury) 46, 55, 71, 79
Harris, Thomas 26, 55 71
Hawkins, Sir John 44, 50, 54
Haym, Nicola Francesco 39
Heidegger, John James 16, 40
'Hickford's Great Room' 40
Hill, Aaron 40, 42
Hogarth, William 43, 44, **45**, 50
Hudson, Thomas 35, 50
Hughes, John 40, 43

J
Jennens, Charles 19, 35, 46, 57, 79–80, **80**

K
Keiser, Reinhard 10, 76, 83
King's Theatre, Haymarket 11, **11**, 16, 17, 18, 23, 40, 65–66

L
Le Lecteur or The Judicious Lover (Hubert Gravelot) **31**
Leipzig 10
Leveridge, Richard 68
Lincoln's Inn Fields Theatre 17

M
MacSwinny, Owen 40, **41**
Mainwaring, [Rev] John 35, 50, 51, 54, 56, 58, 68, 76
Mattheson, Johann 10, **10**, 38, 50, 56
Mercier, Philip 24, 50
Michaelsen, Dorothea Sophie 52

Michaelsen, Michael Dietrich 52, **54**
Middlesex, Lord 18
Milton, John 44, 46, 79
Morell, [Dr] Thomas 46, 55, 80, **83**
Mozart, Wolfgang Amadeus 35, **35**
Music Party, A (Philip Mercier) **63**, **64**

N

Naples 10, 76
Nazari, Bartolomeo 35

O

Opera of the Nobility 16, 40
Ottoboni, Cardinal Pietro 10
Oxford 14

P

Pamphili, Cardinal Benedetto 10, 77
Pantheon, Oxford Street 58
Peg [Margaret] Woffington (artist unknown) **34**
Pendarves, [Mrs] Mary (Mrs Delany) 55, 70–71
Pepusch, John Christopher 39, **39**, 40, 43
Pope, Alexander 42, 43, **43**, 46
Purcell, Henry 42, 68

Q

Queen's Theatre, Haymarket (see King's Theatre)

R

Ranelagh (Pleasure Garden) 41
Reinhold, Henry Theodore, 71
Rich, John 16, **17**, 43
Robinson, Anastasia 69, **69**
Rome 10, 76–77
Roubiliac, Louis François 47, 50–51
Royal Academy of Music 15, 38, 52, 68, 69
Rule, Britannia! 44
Ruspoli, Marquis Francesco Maria 10

S

St George's, Hanover Square 57, **57**
St James's Palace (see also Chapel Royal) 11, 23
St Paul's Cathedral 13
Salisbury 14
Scarborough 14
Senesino [Francesco Bernardi] 16, **16**, 65, **65**, **67**, 68

Shaftesbury, Ashley Cowper, 4th Earl of 55
Smith (the Elder), John Christopher 19, 39, 55, 83, 84
Smith (the younger), John Christopher 19, 39, 55, **82**, 83
Smyth, James 58
Strada [Anna Maria Strada del Pò] 55, 71
Taylor, John 56
Telemann, Georg Philipp 10, 55
Tom's Coffee House, Covent Garden 29, **29**
Tunbridge Wells 14

V

Vanburgh, [Sir] John 40
Vauxhall Pleasure Gardens 14, 41, 47, **47**, 51
Venice 10, 76–77
Walpole, Horace 18
Walpole, [Sir] Robert, 1st Earl of Orford 43
Wesley, Charles 13
Westminster Abbey 19, **19**, 47, 51, 58

Y

York Buildings, Villiers Street 40

Z

Zachow, Friederich Wilhelm 10, 52, 76

Acknowledgements

Particular thanks to the Idlewild Trust for sponsoring this publication; thanks and gratitude to Donald Burrows, John Greenacombe and Anthony Hicks for their support and expertise; the owners of both No. 25 & No. 23 Brook Street, the Co-operative Insurance Society; to our donors, supporters and lenders, both institutions and individuals; the consultants, contractors, craftsmen and women who have worked on the project, in particular Patrick Baty, Dan Cruickshank, Annabel Westman whose expertise has been invaluable to both the refurbishment of the historic interiors and the content of this publication, Jim Hill (A E Chapman's), Gardiner and Theobald (GTMS, GTCM and GT), Context Weavers and the team at K R Hannaford; the picture libraries, in particular the National Portrait Gallery, the photographers, George Garbutt and Matthew Hollow; Caroline Churchill, Emma Conway, Martin Eggelston and Tertia Sefton-Green for their support and good humour; the designer Isambard Thomas and John Fisher (Guildhall Library), Rachel Kennedy, Christopher Purvis and Christine Riding.

Finally, to Stanley and Julie Anne Sadie, without whom this project would never have happened